How to Start & Manage a Cosmetology Business

A Practical Way to Start Your Own Business

By
Jerre G. Lewis and Leslie D. Renn

How to Start & Manage a Cosmetology Business

Lewis & Renn Associates, Inc.

Business & Professional Publishing

10315 Harmony Drive
Interlochen, Michigan 49643
(231) 275-7287

Leslie D. Renn
President

Jerre G. Lewis
Secretary-Treasurer

ISBN # 1-57916-053-0
Library of Congress Catalog Card Number
99-094162

TABLE OF CONTENTS

Chapter 1

Introduction

Selecting the right Cosmetology business opportunity requires careful, thorough evaluations of yourself. Owning your own business is as much a part of the American dream as owning a home, and for you, this urge represents one of life's most exciting challenges. This book is for those men and women who someday may go into business for themselves and for those who are already in business for themselves but wish to strengthen their entrepreneurial and managerial skills.

Entrepreneurs come in all shapes and sizes, personalities, and lifestyles. They are usually highly motivated, hard-working individuals who receive satisfaction from taking risks. Your business should interest you, not just be an income generator. Analyze your personal style. Do you like working with people? Are you a self starter, goal oriented, persistent, a risk taker, willing to work hard and long hours?

If you have been honest in evaluating yourself, you will now select the right type of business. Before you can determine which of the multitude of businesses is right for you to start, you must evaluate the businesses you want to start by asking these questions. Is the business area growing? How does the economy affect it? Who dominates its market? Once you have considered a business that satisfies your needs and interest you must prepare a formal business plan by following the outline given in this book.

Small businesses constitute a dynamic and critical sector of the U.S. economy. Every year in the United States more than 600,000 new businesses are launched by independent men and women eager to make their own decisions, express their own ideas, and be their own bosses. But running your own business is not as easy as it may seem. There can be problems with the inventory, or getting the right goods delivered on time. Yet, managing one's own business can be a personally and financially rewarding experience for an individual strong enough to meet the test. A person with stamina, maturity, and creativity, one who is willing to make sacrifices, may find making a go of a struggling enterprise an exhilarating challenge with many compensations.

Small business owners are a dedicated group of people who work hard and whose hours on the job usually exceed the nine-to-five routine. The owner's commitment is the key to many successful small businesses; an entrepreneur is able to communicate ideas, lead, plan, be patient, and work well with people.

Managing a business requires more than the possession of technical knowledge. Because most small businesses are started by technical people, such as engineers and salesmen, their managerial acumen is often less developed than their technical skills. The need to plan for management is common to every type of and size of business, and there are certain steps that must be taken. Although some of them are very elementary — such as applying for a city business permit — the most important are often complex and difficult and require the advice of specialists: accountants, attorneys, insurance brokers, and/or bankers. For almost any business though, the first step will be to translate the entrepreneur's basic idea into a concrete plan for action.

To gauge your level of entrepreneurial spirit, the following quiz was created. Please answer each question honestly and then total the columns.

ENTREPRENEURIAL QUIZ

	YES	NO	SOMETIMES
1. I am a self-starter. Nobody has to tell me how to get going.	____	____	_____
2. I am capable of getting along with just about everybody.	____	____	_____
3. I have no trouble getting people to follow my lead.	____	____	_____
4. I like to be in charge of things and see them through.	____	____	_____
5. I always plan ahead before beginning a project. I am usually the one who gets everyone organized.	____	____	_____
6. I have a lot of stamina. I can keep going as long as necessary.	____	____	_____
7. I have no trouble making decisions and can make up my mind in a hurry.	____	____	_____
8. I say exactly what I mean. People can trust me.	____	____	_____
9. Once I make my mind up to do something, nothing can stop me.	____	____	_____
10. I am in excellent health and have a lot of energy.	____	____	_____

	YES	NO	SOMETIMES

11. I have experience or technical knowledge in the business I intend to start.

12. I feel comfortable taking risks if it is something I really believe in.

13. I have good communication skills.

14. I am flexible in my dealings with people and situations.

15. I consider myself creative and resourceful.

16. I can analyze a situation and take steps to correct problems.

17. I think I am capable of maintaining a good working relationship with employees.

18. I am not a dictator. I am willing to listen to employees, customers and suppliers.

19. I am not rigid in my policies. I am willing to adjust to meet the needs of employees, customers, and suppliers.

20. More than anything else, I want to run my own business.

Total of Column #1 _____

Total of Column #2 _____

Total of Column #3 _____

If the total of Column #1 is the highest, then you will probably be very successful in running your own business.

If the total of Column #2 is the highest, you may find that running a business is more than you can handle.

If the total of Column #3 is the highest, you should consider taking on a partner who is strong in your weak areas.

NOTE: This quiz was adapted from the Small Business Administration publication *Checklist for Going Into Business.*

Notes _____

Chapter 2

Planning the Business

The Dream of self-employment can be fulfilled. You don't need to finance the opening of an elaborate office or facility to start your own one-person corporation either. You can start your own Cosmetology business.

Anyone preparing to run an Cosmetology business needs to learn a great deal to assure the best possible chance for success.

GETTING STARTED

The following is a list of what you need to accomplish to insure that your Cosmetology endeavor will head in the right direction.

1. Define your educational background and work experience.

2. Survey all the basic types of Cosmetology businesses.

3. Define what products or services your Cosmetology business will be marketing.

4. Define who will be using your products/services.

5. Define why they will be purchasing your products/services.

6. List all competitors in your Cosmetology marketing area.

ZONING REGISTRATIONS

Cosmetology businesses are subject to many laws and regulations enforced by state, county, township governmental units. Most jurisdictions now have codes, a zoning board, and an appeal board which regulate businesses. Areas often are zoned residential, commercial or industrial.

You must become familiar with these regulations. If you are doing business in violation of these regulations, you could be issued a cease and desist order or fined.

Certain kinds of goods cannot be produced in the home, though these restrictions vary somewhat from state-to-state. Most states outlaw home production of fireworks, drugs, poisons, explosives, sanitary/medical products and some toys.

Many localities have registration requirements for new businesses. You will need to obtain a work certificate or license from the state.

TAX REQUIREMENTS

Application for Employer Identification Number, Form SS-4. This registers you with the Internal Revenue Service as a business. If you have employees, you should ask for Circular E along with your ID number. Circular E explains federal income and social security tax withholding requirements.

Employer's Annual Unemployment Tax Return, Form 940. This is only if you have employees. It's used to report and pay the Federal Unemployment Compensation Tax.

Employee's Withholding Allowance Certificate, W-4. Every employee must complete the W-4 so the proper amount of income tax can be withheld from the employee's pay. If the employee claims more than 15 allowances or a complete withholding exemption while having a salary of more than $200 a week, a copy of the W-4 must go to the IRS.

Employer's Wage and Tax Statement, W-2. Used to report to the IRS the total taxes withheld and total compensation paid to each employee per year.

Reconciliation/Transmittal of Income and Tax Statements, W-3. Used to total all information from the W-2. Sent to the Social Security Administration.

The IRS puts on monthly workshops on understanding and using these forms. Call your local IRS office for further information.

States also have various tax form requirements including: an unemployment tax form, a certificate of registration application, a sales and use tax return, an employer's quarterly contribution and payroll report, an income tax withholding registration form, an income tax withholding form, and others. Some forms apply only to employers who have employees. Your local IRS office and state Office of Taxation can provide you with listings of forms you will need to start your business. The following table outlines Federal tax form requirements.

Every small business begins with an idea — a product to be manufactured or sold, a service to be performed.

Whatever the business or its degree of complexity, the owner needs a business plan in order to transform a vision into a working operation.

This business plan should describe in writing and in figures the proposed Cosmetology business and its products, services, or manufacturing processes. It should also include an analysis of the market, a marketing strategy, an organizational plan, and measurable financial objectives.

WHAT SHOULD A BUSINESS PLAN COVER?

It should be a thorough and objective analysis of both personal abilities and business requirements for a particular product or service. It should define strategies for such functions as marketing and production, organization and legal aspects, accounting and finance. A business plan should answer such questions as:

What do I want and what am I capable of doing?
What are the most workable ways of achieving my goals?
What can I expect in the future?

There is no single best way to begin. What follows is simply a guide and can be changed to suit individual needs.

1. Define Long-term goals.
2. State short-term.
3. Set marketing strategies to meet goals and objectives.
4. Analyze available resources.
5. Assemble financial data.
6. Review plan.

Please refer to Figure 2.1 for a complete business plan outline.

The business operator with a realistic plan has the best chance for success.

Figure 2.1

BUSINESS PLAN FOR SMALL BUSINESSES

I.   Type of Business

II.   Location

III.   Target Market

IV.   Planning Process

V.   Organizational Structure

VI.   Staffing Procedures

VII.   Market Strategy

IX.   Financial Planning

X.   Budgeted Balance Sheet

XI.   Budgeted Income Statement

XII.   Budgeted Cash Flow Statement

XIII.   Break-Even Chart

Notes

they will choose the wrong market. Or that other practitioners will take just anybody and therefore some of their business.

You must keep in mind that the purpose of defining your target market is to make your life easier and increase the productivity of your promotional endeavors. Many opportunities exist in this world and it's impossible to pursue them all or be everything to everyone. You need to know where to focus your energy and money when it comes to promotion and advertising.

The two most common means of market analysis are demographics and psychographics, which describe a person in terms of objective data and personality attributes.

Demographics are statistics such as:
- age
- gender
- income level
- geographic location
- occupation
- education level

Psychographics are lifestyle factors including:
- special interest activities
- philosophical beliefs
- social factors
- cultural involvements

The more you know about your potential customers, the easier it is to develop an appropriate position statement and design an effective marketing campaign. The actual number of target markets you have depends mainly upon the size of your practice and the scope of your knowledge.

Chapter 3

Marketing Strategies
for an Cosmetology Business

As a potential Cosmetology business owner, it is important to learn all you can about marketing. You will need to know how to identify your market and how to market your product or service.

As a business person who looks for a profit from the sale of goods, you recognize that without people who want to buy, there is no demand for the things you want to sell. Thus, it is important that, in addition to knowing about the functions of marketing, you also study the activities that will influence the consumer. When you satisfy the specific needs and wants of the customer, then he or she may be willing to pay you a price that will include a profit for you — and to make a profit is one of the reasons you have become an Cosmetology business owner. Although there are many activities connected with marketing, most of them can be classified in these categories: buy, finance, transport, standardize, store, insure, advertise and sell.

Target Market Analysis

Before you can create a successful marketing campaign, it's necessary to determine your target market (toward whom to direct your energies). The whole concept of target marketing can seem very scary at first. On the surface, targeting appears to be limiting the scope of the pool of potential customers. Many people fear that by defining a market, they will lose business. They are concerned that

Defining Your Target Market(s)

Write a descriptive statement for each of your target markets (refer to your "Target Market Profile"). Include a brief overview of the services you are providing to that group and a detailed analysis of the characteristics of the specific clientele.

Target Market 1:

Target Market 2:

Target Market 3:

Your Target Market Profile

In order to clarify your target market(s) you need to delineate the demographic and psychographic factors and then identify the characteristics your customers have in common.

Describe your current customers and those who are most likely your future customers:

What is the age range and average age of your customers?

What is the percentage of males?

What is the percentage of females?

What is the average educational level of your customers?

Where do your customers live?

What are the occupations of your customers?

Where do your customers work?

What is the average annual income level of your customers?

Of what special interest groups are your customers members?

What is the primary reason your customers use your services?

Cosmetology Business Marketing

The foundation for creating a thriving customer base.

A. Overview

   This section is about clarifying your beliefs and attitudes toward your profession and determining the image you wish to portray.

   1. Describe the "character" that you want for your business. Depict the image you want to convey:

   2. State your philosophy in regard to your business:

   3. Describe your philosophy regarding your practice in business:

B. Customer Profile

This is a descriptive analysis of your current and potential customers — who they are, what their interests are, and where you can find them. Include each of your target markets.

1. Target Market 1:

2. Target Market 2:

3. Target Market 3:

C. Competition's Marketing Assessment

The first phase in planning your promotional campaign is appraising the competition. List each of your major competitors and describe the marketing strategies they utilize. Be certain to include where and how often they advertise.

1. Major Competitor 1:

2. Major Competitor 2:

3. Major Competitor 3:

4. Major Competitor 4:

5. Major Competitor 5:

6. Major Competitor 6:

Cosmetology Marketing Planning

Outline for Marketing:

I. Produce/Service Concept
   A. Name of produce or service
   B. Descriptive characteristics of product or service
   C. Unit sales
   D. Analysis of market trends

II. Number of Customers in Market Area:
   A. Profile of customers
   B. Average customer expenditure
   C. Total market

III. Your Market Potential:
   A. Total market divided by competition
   B. Total market multiplied by percent who will buy your product

IV. Needs of Customers:
   A. Identification
   B. Pleasure
   C. Social approval
   D. Personal interest
   E. Price

V. Direct Marketing Sources:
   A. Trade magazines
   B. Trade associates
   C. Small Business Administration (SBA)
   D. Government publications
   E. Yellow Pages
   F. Marketing directories

VI. Customer Profile:
   A. Geographical
   B. Gender
   C. Age range
   D. Income brackets
   E. Occupation
   F. Educational level

Chapter 4

Promoting the Cosmetology Business

When a new business is opened, the owner must be prepared to publicize the business or its chance for success will be slim. Only a few businesses — such as those with a prime location, nationally known name, or a built-in clientele — can succeed without advertising to promote market awareness and stimulate sales.

The first purpose — promoting customer awareness — applies as much to established businesses as to newcomers.

In the Cosmetology business, you will find it easier to retain old customers than to win new ones. When old customers move away from your area, or when their buying needs change, you need new customers to maintain your sales volume. If you expect your business to gain, you will need additional new customers. New customers are those who move into your area or who have grown into your line of products because now they can afford them or they need them. We see advertising and we hear advertising all around us, and yet that is only a part of it. Through advertising, you call the attention of customers to your products.

As a small business owner, you may advertise your business through your location. People pass by and are attracted to your operation because of what you are selling. To get a better idea of what advertising is, consider some of the following functions of advertising:

1. *To inform:* Letting customers know what you have for sale through brochures, leaflets, newspapers, radio, TV, and etc.

2. *Persuade:* Persuasion is the art of leading individuals to do what you want them to do. There are sales personnel who have persuasive sales presentations, but persuasion in advertising is nonpersonal. The appeal is made through the printed or spoken words or a picture. The influence of an ad on readers occurs as purchasers choose what they want among different products, and different wants. To gain the actions you want — a sale — you must persuade a customer to examine personally what you have for sale.

3. *Reminder:* Advertising performs it's third function when it reminds those who have been persuaded to buy once that the same product will bring satisfaction. The ad will also remind a customer of the characteristics of a product purchased some time ago, and where he or she bought it. Because customers change their loyalty to a place of business, their taste for products, and often their trading area patronage, advertising is necessary to draw new customers and to hold old customers. To generate results from advertising that will be profitable to your business, you will have to produce answers to the what, where and how of advertising.

What to Advertise

The nature of your business will partially answer the question "Shall I advertise goods or services?" What are the outstanding features of your business? Is it unique in any way? Does it have strong points? Do you have something to offer that the competition is not able to duplicate? Answers to these questions will give you a start in deciding what to advertise.

Where to Advertise

Of course, you will want to advertise within your marketing area, however there are a few guidelines to remember:

A. Who are your customers?

B. What is their income range?

C. Why do they buy?

D. How do they buy? Do they pay Cash? Charge?

E. What is the radius of your market area?

How to Advertise:

In determining how to advertise, you will have to consider your dollar allocation for advertising and the media suitable to your particular kind of business. However, it is important to have a balance between the presentation of the product or service being advertised and the application of three basic principles.

1. Gain the attention of the audience.

2. Establish a need.

3. Tell where that need may be filled.

See Figure A for an outline of the different advertising media and Figure B for budget on media goals.

Figure A

Advertising Media

Media	Market Coverage	Type of Audience
Daily Newspaper	Single community or entire metro area; zoned editions sometimes available	General
Weekly Newspaper	Single community	Residents
Telephone Directory	Geographical area or occupational field served by the directory	Active shoppers for goods or services
Direct mail audience	Controlled by the advertiser	Controlled
Radio audience	Definable market area	Selected
Television audience	Definable market area	Various
Outdoor	Entire metro area	General auto drivers
Magazine	Entire metro area or magazine region	Selected audience

Figure A

Promotion and Advertising Plan — Cosmetology Business

In designing your promotional plan, it's wise to use a variety of media. You must have specific goals, time lines and budgets for each marketing application

Media	Goal	Timeline	Budget

Notes

Chapter 5

Financial Planning for an Cosmetology Business

Financial planning is the process of analyzing and monitoring the financial performance of your business so you can assess your current position and anticipate future problem areas. The daily, monthly, seasonal, and yearly operation of your business requires attention to the figures that tell you about the firm's financial health.

Maintaining good financial records is a necessary part of doing business.

The increasing number of governmental regulations alone makes it virtually impossible to avoid keeping detailed records. Just as important is to keep them for yourself. The success of your business depends on them. An efficient system of record keeping can help you to:

- make management decisions
- compete in the marketplace
- monitor performance
- keep track of expenses
- eliminate unprofitable merchandise
- protect your assets
- prepare your financial statements

Financial skills should include understanding of the balance sheet, the profit-and-loss statement, cash flow projection, break-even analysis, and source and application of funds. In many businesses, the husband and wife run the business; it is especially important that both of them understand financial management. Most small business owners are not accountants, but they must understand the tool of financial management if they are going to be able to measure the return on their investment. Although good records are essential to good financial planning, they alone are not enough because their full use requires interpretation and analysis. The owner/manager's financial decisions concerning return on invested funds, approaches to banks, securing greater supplier credit, raising additional equity capital and so forth, can be more successful if he takes the time to develop understanding and use of the balance sheet and profit-and-loss statement.

Balance Sheet:

The balance sheet, Figure I, shows the financial condition of a business at the end of business on a specific day. It is called a balance sheet because the total assets balance with, or are equal to, total liabilities plus owner's capital balance. Current assets are those that the owner does not anticipate holding for long. This category includes cash, finished goods in inventory, and accounts receivable. Fixed assets are long-term assets, including plant and equipment. A third possible category is the intangible asset of goodwill. Liabilities are debts owed by the business, including both accounts payable, which are usually short-term, and notes payable, which are usually long-term debts such as mortgage payments. The difference between the value of the assets and the value of the liabilities is the capital. This category includes funds invested by the owner plus accumulated profits, less withdrawals.

The Income Statement:

This statement, Figure II, is also known as a profit-and loss (P&L) statement. It shows how a business has performed over a certain period of time. An income statement specifies sales, costs of sales, gross profit, expenses and net income or loss from operations.

Figure I

Financial Forecast

Opening Balance Sheet - Date

ASSETS

Current Assets

Cash and bank accounts			$
Accounts receivable			$
Inventory			$
Other current assets			$ _____
TOTAL CURRENT ASSETS		(A)	$ _____

Fixed Assets

Property owned			$
Furniture and equipment			$
Business automobile			$
Leasehold improvements			$
Other fixed assets			$ _____
TOTAL FIXED ASSETS		(B)	$ _____
TOTAL ASSETS		(A+B = X)	$ _____

LIABILITIES

Current Liabilities (due within the next 12 months)

Bank loans			$
Other loans			$
Accounts payable			$
Other current liabilities			$ _____
TOTAL CURRENT LIABILITIES		(C)	$ _____

Long-term Liabilities

Mortgages			$
Long-term loans			$
Other long-term liabilities			$ _____
TOTAL LONG-TERM LIABILITIES		(D)	$ _____
TOTAL LIABILITIES		(C+D = Y)	$ _____
NET WORTH		(X-Y = Z)	$ _____
TOTAL NET WORTH AND LIABILITIES		(Y+Z)	$ _____

Figure II

Business Income and Expense Forecast for the Next 12 Months

One year estimate ending _____, 19 _____

Projected Number of Clients

For your services   _____

For your products   _____

TOTAL NUMBER OF CLIENTS   _____

Projected Income

Sessions $ _____

Product sales $ _____

Other $ _____

TOTAL INCOME $ _____

Projected Expenses

Start-up costs $ _____

Monthly expenses (x 12) $ _____

Annual expenses $ _____

TOTAL EXPENSES $ _____

TOTAL OPERATING PROFIT (OR LOSS) $ _____

CAPITAL REQUIRED FOR THE NEXT 12 MONTHS $ _____

Cosmetology Business

Start-Up Costs Worksheet	
Item	**Estimated Expense**
Open checking account	$
Telephone installation	$
Equipment	$
First & last month's rent, security deposit, etc.	$
Supplies	$
Business cards, stationery, etc.	$
Advertising and promotion package	$
Decorating and remodeling	$
Furniture and fixtures	$
Legal and professional fees	$
Insurance	$
Utility deposits	$
Beginning inventory	$
Installation of fixtures and equipment	$
Licenses and permits	$
Other	$
TOTAL	$

Fixed Annual Expense Worksheet	
Item	**Estimated Expense**
Property insurance	$
Business auto insurance	$
Licenses and permits	$
Liability insurance	$
Disability insurance	$
Professional society membership	$
Fees (legal, accounting, etc.)	$
Taxes	$
Other	$
TOTAL	$

Monthly Business Expense Worksheet		
Expense	**Estimated Monthly Cost**	**X 12**
Rent	$	$
Utilities	$	$
Telephone	$	$
Bank fees	$	$
Supplies	$	$
Stationery and business cards	$	$
Networking club dues	$	$
Education (seminars, books professional journals, etc.)	$	$
Business car (Payments, gas, repairs, etc)	$	$
Advertising and promotion	$	$
Postage	$	$
Entertainment	$	$
Repair, cleaning and maintenance	$	$
Travel	$	$
Business loan payments	$	$
Salary/Draw	$	$
Staff salaries	$	$
Miscellaneous	$	$
Taxes	$	$
Professional fees	$	$
Decorations	$	$
Furniture and fixtures	$	$
Equipment	$	$
Inventory	$	$
Other	$	$
TOTAL MONTHLY	$	$
TOTAL YEARLY		$

	Cash Flow Forecast					
	January Estimate	January Actual	February Estimate	February Actual	March Estimate	March Actual
Beginning cash						
Plus monthly income from: Fees						
Sales						
Loans						
Other						
TOTAL CASH AND INCOME						
Expenses:						
Rent						
Utilities						
Telephone						
Bank fees						
Supplies						
Stationery and business cards						
Insurance						
Dues						
Education						
Auto						
Advertising and promotion						
Postage						
Entertainment						

	January Estimate	January Actual	February Estimate	February Actual	March Estimate	March Actual
Cash Flow Forecast (Continued)						
Repair and maintenance						
Travel						
Business loan payments						
Licenses and permits						
Salary/Draw						
Staff salaries						
Taxes						
Professional fees						
Decorations						
Furniture and fixtures						
Equipment						
Inventory						
Other Expenses						
TOTAL EXPENSES						
ENDING CASH (+/-)						

Notes

Chapter 6

Cosmetology Business Planning

Introduction

Our increasingly service oriented economy offers a widening spectrum of opportunities for customized and personalized small business growth. Though untrained entrepreneurs have traditionally had a high rate of failure, small businesses can be profitable. Success in a small Cosmetology business is not an accident. It requires both skills in a service or product area and acquisition of management and attitudinal competencies.

The purpose of this publication is to help you take stock of your interests, aptitudes and skills. Many people have good business ideas but not everyone has what it takes to succeed. If you are convinced that a profitable Cosmetology business is attainable, this publication will provide step-by-step guidance in development of the basic written business plan.

Information Gathering

A helpful tool for use in determining if you are ready to take the risks of an Cosmetology business operation is the SMA publication entitled *Going Into Business* (MP-12).

It will help you focus on the basic steps in information gathering and business planning.

Careful planning is required to research legal and tax issues, proper space utilization and to establish time management discipline. Inadequate or careless attention to development of a detailed business plan can be costly for you and your family in terms of lost time, wasted talent and disappearing dollars.

The Entrepreneurial Personality

A variety of experts have documented research that indicates that successful small business entrepreneurs have some common characteristics. How do you measure up? On this checklist, write a "Y" if you believe the statement describes you; a "N" if it doesn't; and a "U" if you can't decide:

_____   I have a strong desire to be my own boss.

_____   Win lose or draw, I want to be master of my own financial destiny.

_____   I have significant specialized business ability based on both my education and my experience.

_____   I have an ability to conceptualize the whole of a business; not just its individual parts, but how they relate to each other.

_____   I develop an inherent sense of what is "right" for a business and have the courage to pursue it.

_____   One or both of my parents were entrepreneurs; calculate risk-taking runs in the family.

_____   My life is characterized by a willingness and capacity to preserver.

_____   I possess a high level of energy, sustainable over long hours to make the business successful.

While not every successful Cosmetology business owner starts with a "Y" answer to all of these questions, three or four "N"s and "U"s should be sufficient reason for you to stop and give a second thought to going it alone. Many proprietors who sense entrepreneurial deficiencies seek extra training a support their limitations with help from a skilled team of business advisors such as accountants, bankers and attorneys.

Selecting a Business

A logical first step for the undecided is to list potential areas of personal background, special training, education and job experience, and special interests that could be developed into a business. Review the following list of activities which have proven marketable for others. On a scale of "0" (no interest or strength) to "10" (maximum interest or strength) indicate the potential for you and a total score for each activity.

Time Management

For both the novice and the experienced business person planning a small Cosmetology enterprise, an early concern requiring self-evaluation is time management.

It is very difficult for some people to make and keep work schedules even in a disciplined office setting. As your own boss the problem can be much greater. To determine how much time you can devote to your business, begin by drafting a weekly task timetable listing all current and potential responsibilities and the blocks of time required for each. When and how can business responsibilities be added without undue physical or mental stress on you or your family? Potential conflicts must be faced and resolved at the outset and as they occur, otherwise your business can become a nightmare. During the first year of operation, continue to chart, post and checkoff tasks on a daily, weekly and monthly basis.

Distractions and excuses for procrastination abound. It is important to keep both a planning and operating log. These tools will help avoid oversights and provide vital information when memory fails.

To improve the quality of work time, consider installation of a telephone line for the business and attaching an answering machine to take messages when you do not wish to be distracted or are away from your business. A business line has the added advantage of allowing you to have a business listing in the phone book and if you wish to buy it, an ad in the classified directory.

Is an Cosmetology Business Site Allowable?

Now you will want to investigate potential legal and community problems associated with operating the business. You should gather, read and digest specialized information concerning federal, state, county and municipal laws and regulations concerning Cosmetology business operations.

Check first! Get the facts in writing. Keep a topical file for future reference. Some facts and forms will be needed for your business plan. There may be limitations enforced that can make your planned business impossible or require expensive modifications to your property.

Items to be investigated, recorded and studied are:

TO DO   DONE

TO DO	DONE	
_____	_____	county or city zoning code restrictions
_____	_____	necessary permits and licenses for operation
_____	_____	state and local laws and codes regarding zoning
_____	_____	deed or lease restrictions such as covenants and restrictive conditions of purchase

_____	_____	parking and customer access; deliveries
_____	_____	sanitation, traffic and noise codes
_____	_____	signs and advertising
_____	_____	state and federal code requirements for space, ventilation, heat and light
_____	_____	limitations on the number and type of workers. If not, check with the local Chamber of Commerce office
_____	_____	reservations that neighbors may have about a business next to or near them

Here are some ways to collect your information. Call or visit the zoning office at county headquarters or city hall. In some localities the city or county Office of Economic Development has print materials available to pinpoint key "code" items affecting a business.

Even in rural areas, the era of unlimited free enterprise is over. Although the decision makers may be in the state capital or in a distant regional office of a federal agency, check before investing in inventory, equipment or marketing programs. If in doubt, call the state office of Industrial Development or the nearest SBA district office. In some states the county agent or home demonstration agent will have helpful information concerning rural or farm business development.

Is the Business Site Insurable?

In addition to community investigations, contact your insurance company or agent. It is almost certain that significant changes will be required in your coverage and limits when you start a business. When you have written a good description of your business, call your agent for help in insuring you properly against new hazards resulting from your business operations such as:

37

- Fire, theft and casualty damage to inventories and equipment
- business interruption coverage
- fidelity bonds for employees
- liability for customers, vendors and others visiting the business
- workmen's compensation
- group health and life insurance
- product liability coverage if you make or sell a product; workmanship liability for services
- business use of vehicle coverage

Overall Cosmetology Site Evaluation

After you have gathered as much information as seems practical you may wish to evaluate several different locations. Here's a handy checklist. Using the "0" to "10" scale, grade these vital factors:

Factors to Consider

Factor   **Grades 0-10**

1. Customer convenience
   _____

2. Availability of merchandise or raw materials
   _____

3. Nearby competition
   _____

4. Transportation availability and rates
   _____

5. Quality and quantity of employees available
   _____

6. Availability of parking facilities

7. Adequacy of utilities (sewer, water, power, gas)   _____

8. Traffic flow   _____

9. Tax burden   _____

10. Quality of police and fire services   _____

11. Environmental factors   _____

12. Physical suitability for future expansion   _____

13. Provision for future expansion   _____

14. Vendor delivery access   _____

15. Personal convenience   _____

16. Cost of operation   _____

17. Other factors including how big you get without moving   _____

TOTALS   _____

Writing the Business Plan

Now that your research and plan development is nearing completion, it is time to move into action. If you are still in favor of going ahead, it is time to take several specific steps. The key one is to organize your dream scheme into a business plan.

What is it?

- As a business plan it is written by the Cosmetology business owner with outside help as needed
- It is accurate and concise as a result of careful study
- It explains how the business will function in the marketplace
- It clearly depicts its operational characteristics
- It details how it will be financed
- It outlines how it will be managed
- It is the management and financial "blueprint" for start-up and profitable operation
- It serves as a prospectus for potential investors and lenders

Why create it?

- The process of putting the business plan together, including the thought that you put in before writing it, forces you to take an objective, critical, unemotional look at your entire business proposal
- The finished written plan is an operational tool which, when properly used, will help you manage your business and work toward its success
- The completed business plan is a means for communicating your ideas to others and provides the basis for financing your business

Who should write it?

- The Cosmetology owner to the extend possible
- Seek assistance in weak areas, such as:
  - accounting
  - insurance
  - capital requirements
  - operational forecasting
  - tax and legal requirements

When should a business plan be used?

- To make crucial start-up decisions
- To reassure lenders or backers
- To measure operations progress
- To test planning assumptions
- As a basis for adjusting forecasts
- To anticipate ongoing capital and cash requirements
- As the benchmark for good operations management

Proposed Outline for Cosmetology Business Plan

This outline is suggested for a small proprietorship or family business. Shape it to fit *your* unique needs. For more complex manufacturing or franchise operations see the Resource section for other options.

Part I - Business Organization

Cover page:

    A.   Business name:

            Street address:

            Mailing address:

            Telephone number:

            Owner(s) name(s):

Inside pages:

    B.   Business form:

            (proprietorship, partnership, corporation)

            If incorporated (state incorporation)

            Include copies of key subsidiary documents in an appendix.

Remember even partnerships require written agreements of terms and conditions to avoid later conflicts and to establish legal entities and equities. Corporations require charters, articles of incorporation and bylaws.

Part II - Business Purpose and Function

In this section, write an accurate yet, concise description of the business. Describe the business you plan to start in narrative form.

What is the principal activity? Be specific. Give product or service description(s):

- retail sales?

- manufacturing?

- service?

- other?

How will it be started?

- a new start up

- the expansion of an existing business

- purchase of a going business

- a franchise operation

- actual or projected start up date

Why will it succeed? Promote your idea!

- how and why this business will be successful

- what is unique about your business

- what is its market "niche"

What is your experience in this business? If you have a current resume of your career, include it in an appendix and reference it here. Otherwise write a narrative here and include a resume in the finished product. If you lack specific experience, detail how you plan to gain it, such as training, apprenticeship or working with partners who have experience.

The Marketing Plan

The marketing plan is the core of your business rationale. To develop a consistent sales growth an Cosmetology business person much become knowledgeable about the market. To demonstrate your understanding, this section of the Cosmetology business plan should seek to concisely answer several basic questions:

Who is your market?

- Describe the profile of your typical customer

    Age?

    Male, female, both?

    How many in family?

    Annual family income?

    Location?

    Buying patterns?

    Reason to buy from you?

Other?

- Biographically describe your trading area (i.e., county, state, national)

- Economically describe your trading area: (single family, average earnings, number of children)

How large is the market?

- Total units or dollars?

- Growing _____ Steadily _____ Decreasing _____

- If growing, annual growth rate. _____

Who is your competition?

No small business operates in a vacuum. Get to know and respect the competition. Target your marketing plans. Identify direct competitors (both in terms of geography and product lines), and those who are similar or marginally comparative. Begin by listing names, addresses and products or service. Detail briefly but concisely the following information concerning each of your competitors:

- Who are the nearest ones?

- How are their businesses similar or competitive to yours?

- Do you have a unique "niche"? Describe it.

- How will your service or product be better or more saleable than your competitors?

- Are their businesses growing? Stable? Declining? Why?

- What can be learned from observing their operations or talking to their present or former clients?

- Will you have competitive advantages or disadvantages? Be honest!

What percent of the market will you penetrate?

1. estimate the market in total units or dollars

2. estimate your planned volume

3. amount your volume will add to total market

4. subtract 3 from 2

Item 4 represents the amount of your planned volume that must be taken away from the competition.

What pricing and sales terms are you planning?

The primary consideration in pricing a product or service is the value that it represents to the customer. If, on the previous checklist of features, your product is truly ahead of the field, you can command a premium price. On the other hand, if it is a "me too" product, you may have to "buy" a share of the market to get your foothold and then try to move price up later. This is always risky and difficult. One rule will always hold: ultimately, the market will set the price. If your selling price does not exceed your costs and expenses by the margin necessary to keep your business healthy, you will fail. Know your competitors pricing policies. Send a friend to comparison shop. Is there discounting? Special sales? Price leaders? Make some "blind" phone calls. Detail your pricing policy.

What is your sales plan?

Describe how you will sell, distribute or service what you sell. Be specific. Below are outlined some common practices:

Direct Sales - by telephone or in person. The tremendous growth of individual sales representatives who sell by party bookings, door to door, and through distribution of call back promotional campaigns suggests that careful research is required to be profitable.

Mail Order - Specialized markets for leisure time or unique products have grown as more two income families find less time to shop. Be aware of recent mail order legislation and regulation.

Franchising -

a. You may decide to either buy into someone else's franchise as a franchisee, or

b. Create your own franchise operation that sells rights to specific territories or product lines to others. Each will require further legal, financial and marketing research.

Management Plan

Who will do what?

Be sure to include four basic sets of information:

1. State a personal history of principals and related work, hobby or volunteer experience (include formal resumes in Appendix)

2. List and describe specific duties and responsibilities of each

3. List benefits and other forms of compensation for each

4. Identify other professional resources available to the business: Example: Accountant, lawyer, insurance broker, banker. Describe relationship of each to business: Example "Accountant available on part-time hourly basis, as needed, initial agreement calls for services not to exceed x hours per month at $xx.xx per hour."

To make this section graphically clear, start with a simple organizational chart that lists specific tasks and shows, *who* (type of person is more important than an individual name other than for principals) will do *what* indicate by arrows, work flow and lines of responsibility and/or communications. Consider the following examples:

or like this?

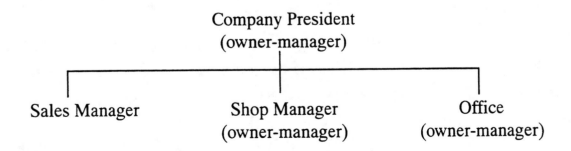

As the service business grows, its organization chart could look like this:

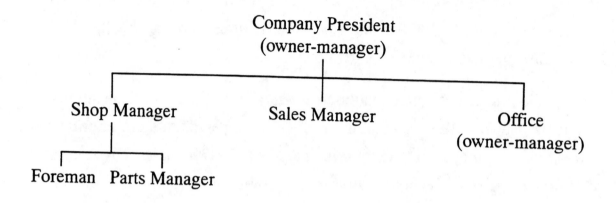

The Financial Plan

Clearly the most critical section of your business plan document is the financial plan. In formulating this part of the planning document, you will establish vital schedules that will guide the financial health of your business through the troubled waters of the first year and beyond.

Before going into the details of building the financial plan, it is important to realize that some basic knowledge of accounting is essential to the productive management of your business. If you are like most business owners, you probably have a deep and abiding interest in the product or services that you sell or intend to sell. You like to do what you do, and it is even more fulfilling that you are making money doing it. There is nothing wrong with that. Your conviction that what you are doing or making is worthwhile is vitally important to success. Nonetheless, the income of a coach who takes the greatest pride in producing a winning team will largely depend on someone keeping score of the wins and losses.

The business owner is no different. Your product or service may improve the condition of mankind for generations to come, but, unless you have access to an unlimited bankroll, you will fail if you don't make a profit. If you don't know what's going on in your business, you are not in a very good position to assure its profitability.

Most Cosmetology businesses will use the "cash" method of accounting with a system of record keeping that may be little more than a carefully annotated checkbook in which is recorded all receipts and all expenditures, backed up by a few forms of original entry (invoices, receipts, cash tickets). For a Sole Partnership, the business form assumed by this Management Aid, the very minimum of recorded information is that required to accurately complete the Federal Internal Revenue Service Form 1040, Schedule C. Other business types (partnerships, joint ventures, corporations) have similar requirements but use different tax forms.

If your business is, or will be, larger than just a small supplement to family income, you will need something more sophisticated. Stationery stores can provide you with several packaged small business account systems complete with simple journals and ledgers and detailed instructions in understandable language.

Should you feel that your accounting knowledge is so rudimentary that you will need professional assistance to establish your accounting system, the classified section of your telephone directory can lead you to a number of small business services that offer a complete range of accounting services. You can buy as much as you need, from a simple "pegboard" system all the way to computerized accounting, tax return service and monthly profitability consultation. Rates are reasonable for the services rendered and an investigative consultation will usually be free. Look under the heading, "Business Consultants," and make some calls.

Let's start by looking at the makeup of the financial plan for the business.

The Financial plan includes the following:

1. Financial Planning Assumptions - these are short statements of the conditions under which you plan to operate.

- Market health
- Date of start-up
- Sales build-up ($)
- Gross profit margin
- Equipment, furniture and fixtures required
- Payroll and other key expenses that will impact the financial plan

2. Operations Plan - Profit and Loss Projection - this is prepared for the first year's Budget. Appendix A-11.

3. Source of Funds Schedule - this shows the source(s) of your funds to capitalize the business and how they will be distributed among your fixed assets and working capital.

4. Pro Forma Balance Sheet - "Pro forma" refers to the fact that the balance sheet is before the fact, not actual. This form displays Assets, Liabilities and Equity of the business. This will indicate how much Investment will be required by the business and how much of it will be used as Working Capital in its operation.

5. Cash Flow Projection - this will forecast the flow of cash into and out of your business through the year. It helps you plan for staged purchasing, high volume months and slow periods.

Creating the Profit and Loss Projection.

Appendix A-11. Create a wide sheet of analysis paper with a three inch wide column at the extreme left and thirteen narrow columns across the page. Write at the top of the first page the planned name of your business. On the second line of the heading, write "Profit and Loss Projection." On the third line, write "First Year."

Then, note the headings on Appendix A-11 and copy them onto your 12-column sheet, copy the headings from the similar area on Exhibit A. Then follow the example set by Appendix A-11 and list all of the other components of your income, cost and expense structure. You may add or delete specific loans of expense to suit your business plan. Guard against consolidating too many types of expenses under one account lest you lose control of the components. At the same time, don't try to break down expenses so discretely that accounting becomes a nuisance instead of a management tool. Once again, Exhibit A provides ample detail for most businesses.

Now, in the small column just to the left of the first monthly column, you will want to note which of the items in the left-hand column are to be estimated on a monthly (M) or yearly (Y) basis. Items such as Sales, Cost of Sales and Variable expenses will be estimated monthly based on planned volume and seasonal or other estimated fluctuations. Fixed Expenses can usually be estimated on a yearly basis and divided by twelve to arrive at even monthly values. The "M" and "Y" designations will be used later to distinguish between variable and fixed expense.

Depreciation allowances for Fixed Assets such as production equipment, office furniture and machines, vehicles, etc. will be calculated from the Source of Funds Schedule.

Appendix A-11 describes line by line how the values on the Profit and Loss Projection are developed. Use this as your guide.

Source of Funds Schedule
To create this schedule, you will need to create a list of all the Assets that you intend to use in your business, how much investment each will require and the source of funds to capitalize them. A sample of such a list is shown below:

Asset	Cost	Source of Funds
Cash	$2,500	Personal savings
Accounts Receivable	3,000	From profits
Inventory	2,000	Vendor credit
Pickup truck	5,000	Currently owned
Packaging machine	10,000	Installment purchase
Office desk and chair	300	Currently owned
Calculator	75	Personal cash
Electric typewriter*	500	Personal savings

* A note about office equipment, test use or rent two or more brands that appear to meet your needs and select the one with which you feel most comfortable. Don't be afraid to ask others who have had to make this decision for advice. Compatibility of your system with those of potential typesetting services or printers should be of high considerations. If you are not quite sure, consider renting or leasing the equipment until you are. Service contracts on such complex electronic gear are usually a good insurance policy.

Before you leave your Source of Funds Schedule, indicate the number of months (years x 12) of useful life for depreciable fixed assets. (An example, the pickup truck, the packaging machine and the furniture and office equipment would be depreciable.) Generally, any individual item of equipment, furniture, fixtures, vehicles, etc., costing over $100 should be depreciated. For more information on allowances for depreciation, you can get free publications and assistance from your local Internal Revenue Service office. Divided the cost of each fixed asset item by the number or months over which it will be depreciated. You will need this data to enter as monthly depreciation on your Profit and Loss Projection. All of the data on the Source of Funds Schedule will be needed to create the Balance Sheet.

Creating the Pro Forma Balance Sheet

Appendix A-13. This is the Balance Sheet Form. There are a number of variations of this form and you may find it prudent to ask your banker for the form that the bank uses for small business. It will make it easier for them to evaluate the health of your business. Use this to get started and transfer the data to your preferred form later. Accompanying Appendix A-12 which describes line by line how to develop the Balance Sheet.

Even though you may plan to stage the purchase of some assets through the year, for the purpose of this pro forma Balance Sheet, assume that all assets will be provided at the start-up.

Cash Flow Projection

An important subsidiary schedule to your financial plan is a monthly Cash Flow Projection. Prudent business management practice is to keep no more cash in the business than is needed to operate it and to protect it from catastrophe. In most small businesses, the problem is rarely one of having too much cash. A Cash Flow Projection is made to advise management of the amount of cash that is going to be absorbed by the operation of the business and compares it against the amount that will be available.

SBA has created an excellent form for this purpose and it is shown as Appendix B. Your projection should be prepared on 13-column analysis paper to allow for a twelve-month projection. Appendix B represents a line by line description and explanation of the components of the Cash Flow Projection which provides a step-by-step method of preparation.

Resources

U.S. Small Business Administration
Office of Business Development

Business Development Publication
MP15

Cosmetology Business

American Beauty Association (ABA)
401 N. Michigan Ave.
Chicago, IL 60611
Paul Dykstra, Exec. Dir.
PH: (312) 644-6610   FX: (312) 245-1080
Founded: 1985   Members: 200

Association of Cosmetologists and Hairdressers (ACH)
1811 Monroe
Dearborn, MI 48124
Mary Ann Neuman, Pres.
PH: (313) 563-0360   FX: (313) 563-0360
Founded: 1985   Members: 3,150

National Cosmetology Association (NCA)
3510 Olive St.
St. Louis, MO 63103
PH: (314) 534-7980
TF: (800) 527-1683   FX: (314) 534-8618
Founded: 1921   Members: 40,000

Hair International/Associated Master Barbers and Beauticians of America (HI/AMBBA)
124-B E. Main St.
P.O. Box 273
Palmyra, PA 17078
Desiree Roberts, Office Mgr.
PH: (717) 838-0795   FX: (717) 838-0796
Founded: 1924   Members: 1,000

Notes

Chapter 7

Managing The Business

Delegating work, responsibility, and authority is difficult in a small business because it means letting others make decisions which involved spending the owner/manager's money. At a minimum, he should delegate enough authority to get the work done, to allow assistants to take initiative, and to keep the operation moving in his absence. Coaching those who carry responsibility and authority in self-improvement is essential and emphasis in allowing competent assistants to perform in their own style rather than insisting that things be done exactly as the owner/manager would personally do them is important. "Let others take care of the details" is the meaning of delegating work and responsibility. In theory, the same principles for getting work done through other people apply whether you have 25 employees and one top assistant or 150 to 200 employees and several keymen yet, putting the principles into practice is often difficult.

Delegation is perhaps the hardest job owner/managers have to learn. Some never do. They insist on handling many details and work themselves into early graves. Others pay lip service to the idea but actually run a one-man shop. They give their assistants many responsibilities but little or no authority. Authority is the fuel that makes the machine go when you delegate word and responsibility. If an owner/manager is to run a successful company, he must delegate authority properly. How much authority is proper depends on your situation. At a minimum, you should delegate enough authority: (1) to get the work done, (2) to allow keymen to take initiative, (3) to keep things going in your absence.

The person who fills a key management spot in the organization must either be a manager or be capable of becoming one. A manager's chief job is to plan, direct, and coordinate the work of others. He should possess the three "I's" — Initiative, Interest, and Imagination. The manager of a department must have enough self-drive to start and keep things moving. Personality traits must be considered. A keyman should be strong-willed enough to overcome opposition when necessary.

When you manage through others, it is essential that you keep control. You do it by holding a subordinate responsible for his actions and checking the results of those actions. In controlling your assistants, try to strike a balance. You should not get into a keyman's operations so closely that you are "in his hair" nor should you be so far removed that you lose control of things.

You need feedback to keep yourself informed. Reports provide a way to get the right kind of feedback at the right time. This can be daily, weekly, or monthly depending on how soon you need the information. Each department head can report his progress, or lack of it, in the unit of production that is appropriate for his activity; for example, items packed in the shipping room, sales per territory, hours of work per employee.

For the owner/manager, delegation does not end with good control. It involves coaching as well, because management ability is not required automatically. You have to teach it. Just as important, you have to keep your managers informed just as you would be if you were doing their jobs.

Part of your job is to see that they get the facts they need for making their decisions. You should be certain that you convey your thinking when you coach your assistants. Sometimes words can be inconsistent with thoughts. Ask questions to make sure that the listener understands your meaning. In other words, delegation can only be effective when you have good communications.

Sometimes an owner/manager finds himself involved in many operational details even though he does everything that is necessary for delegation of responsibility. In spite of defining authority, delegation, keeping control, and coaching, he is still burdened with detailed work. Usually, he had failed to do one vital thing. He has refused to stand back and let the wheels turn.

If the owner/manager is to make delegation work, he must allow his subordinates freedom to do things their way. He and the company are in trouble if he tries to measure his assistants by whether they do a particular task exactly as he would do it. They should be judged by their results — not their methods. No two persons react exactly the same in every situation. Be prepared to see some action taken differently from the way in which you would do it even though your policies are well defined. Of course, if an assistant strays too far from policy, you need to bring him back in line. You cannot afford second-guessing.

You should also keep in mind that when an owner/manager second-guesses his assistants, he risks destroying their self-confidence. If the assistant does not run his department to your satisfaction and if his shortcomings cannot be overcome, then replace him. But when results prove his effectiveness, it is good practice to avoid picking at each move he makes.

Notes

Chapter 8

Business Resource Information

Books   *Anatomy of a Business Plan.* Linda Pinson and Jerry Jennett. Fullerton, CA: Out of Your Mind… and Into the Marketplace, 1988.

How to Borrow Money from a Bank. Don H. Alexander. New York: Beaufort Books, 1984.

Basic Accounting for the Small Business. Clive G. Cornish. Seattle: Self-Counsel Press, Inc., 1984.

Becoming Self-Employed: First Hand Advice from Those Who Have Done It. Susan Elliott. Blue Ridge, PA: Liberty (a division of TAB Books), 1987.

The Business Planning Guide: Creating a Plan for Success in Your Own Business. David H. Bangs, Jr. Dover, NH: Upstart Publishing Company, 1988.

The Complete No Nonsense Success Library. Steve Kahn. Stamford, Conn.: Longmeadow Press.

Complete Start-Up Kit for a Business with Your Computer. Paul and Sarah Edwards. Santa Monica, CA: Here's How, 1989.

Consultant's Kit: Establishing and Operating Your Successful Consulting Business. Jeffrey L. Lant. Cambridge, MA: Jeffrey L. Lant Associates, 1981.

Developing Target Markets. John H. Melchinger. Southborough, MA: Educational Training Systems, Inc.

Directory of Online Databsses. Santa Monica, CA: Caudra Associates, Inc. (Published quarterly).

Do What You Love-The Money Will Follow. Marsha Sinetar. New York: Paulist Press, 1987.

Entrepreneurial Mothers. Phyllis Gillis. New York: Rawson Associates, 1984.

How to Prosper in Your Own Business-Getting Started and Staying on Course. Brian R. Smith. Brattleboro, VT: The Stephen Green Press, 1981.

How to Run a Small Business. J.K. Lasser, ed. Manchester, MO: McGraw-Hill Book Company, 1988.

How to Start a Profitable Child Care Program in Your Home. Patricia Gallagher. Worcester, PA: Child Care and You.

How to Start a Successful Word Processing Business in Your Home. Penny McBride. P.O. Box 2133, Leucadia, CA 92024.

How to Start Your Own Bed and Breakfast: A Guide to Hosting Paying Guests in Your House or Apartment. Mary Zander. Spencertown, NY: Golden Hill Press, 1985.

Ideal to Marketplace: An Investor's Guide. Thomas R.
Lampe. Los Angeles: Price Stern Sloan, 1988.

The Loan Package. Emmett Ramey and Alex Wong.
Sunnyvale, CA: Successful Business Library, 1982.

Managing the One-Person Business. Mary Jean Parson. New
York: Dodd, Mead, 1987.

Marketing: Researching and Reaching Your Target Market.
Linda Pinson and Jerry Jennett. Fullerton, CA: Out of Your
Mind and... Into the Marketplace, 1988.

Marketing without Advertising; Michail Phillips and Salli
Rasberry. Laytonville, CA: In Business Bookshelf, 1986.

Marketing Your Product. Douglas A. Gray and Donald Cyr.
Seattle: Self-Counsel Press Inc., 1987.

Marketing Your Service. Jean Withers and Carol Vipperman.
Seattle: Self-Counsel Press Inc., 1987.

Periodicals

Business Week
1221 Avenue of the Americas
New York, NY 10020
or
P.O. Box 430
Highstown, NJ 08520

Entrepreneur
2311 Pontius Avenue
Los Angeles, CA 90064

Fortune
1271 Avenue of the Americas
New York, NY 10020

The Futurist
The World Future Society
4916 St. Elmo Avenue
Bethesda, MD 20814

Harvard Business Review
P.O. Box 3000
Woburn, MA 01888

In Business
Box 351
Emmaus, PA 18049

INC.
36 Commercial Warf Road
Boston, MA 02166

Info World
375 Cochituate Road
Fromingham, MA 01701

Modern Office Procedures
1111 Chester Avenue
Cleveland, OH 44114

Mother Earth News
P.O. Box 70
Hendersonville, NC 28739

Nation's Business
4940 Nicholson Court
Kensington, MD 20895

Newsweek
444 Madison Avenue
New York, NY 10022

The Office
1200 Summer Street
Stamford, CT 06904

Savvy
P.O. Box 2495
Boulder, CO 80322

Success
P.O. Box 33000
Bergenfield, NH 07621

Technology Review
MIT
Room 10-140
Cambridge, MA 02139

U.S. News and World Report
2300 N Street, N.W.
Washington, DC 20037

Venture
P.O. Box 3206
Harlan, IA 51537

Working Woman
342 Madison Avenue
New York, NY 10017
or
P.O. Box 10130
Des Moines, IA 50349

Mothering
P.O. Box 1690
Santa Fe, NM 87504

Direct Response Specialist
   P.O. Box 1075
   Tarpon Springs, FL 34286
   (813) 937-3480
   Monthly

Family Business Review
   Family Firm Institute
   P.O. Box 476
   Johnstown, NY 12095
   (518) 762-2853
   Bimonthly

Long Island Freelance Network
   (a division of the National
   Freelance Network)
   415 Rutgers Road

West Babylon, NY 11704
(516) 422-9010
Bimonthly

Minding Your Own Business
   John H. Melchinger Company
   15 Cypress Street
   Suite 207
   Newton Centre, MA 02159-2231
   (617) 969-0823
   Bimonthly

Newsletters

Challenges
   P.O. Box 22432
   Kansas City, MO 64113-2432
   (816) 363-6544
   7 times per year

Direct Response Specialist
   P.O. Box 1075
   Tarpon Springs, FL 34286
   (813) 937-3480
   Monthly

Family Business Review
   Family Firm Institute
   P.O. Box 476
   Johnstown, NY 12095
   (518) 762-2853
   Bimonthly

Freelance Journal
   7507 Sunset Boulevard
   Suite 213
   Los Angeles, CA 90046
   (213) 874-8281
   Bimonthly

Home Business Advisor
NextStep Publications
P.O. Box 41108
Fayetteville, NC 28309
(919) 867-2128

Home Business Advocate
Wendy Priesnitz and Associates
195 Markville Road
Unionville, Ontario
Canada L3R4V8

Home Business Line
397 Post Road
Darien, CT 06820
(203) 655-4380
Monthly

Home Business Monthly
38 Briarcliffe Road
Rochester, NY 14617
(716) 338-1144
Bimonthly

American Small Business
Association
P.O. Box 612663
Dallas, TX 75261
(800) 227-1037

American Society of Independent
Business
777 Main Street, Suite 1600
Fort Worth, TX 76102
(917) 870-1880

Assn of Small Business Dev. Centers
1313 Farnam, Suite 132
Omaha, NE 68182
(402) 595-2387

Best Employers Association
4201 Birch Street
Newport Beach, CA 92660
(714) 756-6100

Chexchange Network
P.O. Box 21697
Columbus, OH 21697
(614) 292-4985

Coalition of Women in National and
Int'l Business
P.O. Box 950
Boston, MA 02119
(617) 265-5269

Continental Assn of Resolute
Employers
101 Petaluma Boulevard N
Petaluma, CA 94952
(707) 778-8600

Int'l Council of Small Business
3674 Lindell Boulevard
St. Louis, MO 63108
(314) 658-3896

Nat'l Assn of Small Business
Investment Companies
1199 N. Fairfax St, Suite 200
Alexandria, VA 22314
(703) 683-1601

Nat'l Assn of Home Based
  Businesses
10451 Mill Run Circle, Suite 40
Owings Mills, MD 21117
(410) 363-3698

Nat'l Business Incubation Assn
  20 E. Circle Dr., Suite 190
  Athens, OH 45701

National Alliance of Small Business
  1825 Eye Street NW, Suite 400
  Washington, DC 20077-2740

National Assn for Business Org.
  P.O. Box 30149
  Baltimore, MD 21270
  (301) 446-8070

National Assn for Female Executives
  127 W. 24th Street
  New York, NY 10011
  (212) 645-0770

National Small Business Association
  1640 K Street NW
  Washington, DC 20006
  (202) 293-8830

Network of Small Business
  5420 Mayfield Road, Suite 205
  Lyndhurst, OH 44124
  (216) 442-5000

Public Information Department New
  York Federal Reserve Bank
  33 Liberty St.
  New York, NY 10045

Service Corps of Retired Executives
  1825 Connecticut Ave., NW,
  Suite 503
  Washington, DC 20009
  (800) 368-5855

Small Business Assistance Center
  P.O. Box 1441
  Worchester, MA 01601
  (508) 756-3513

Small Business Foundation of
  America Research Inst. for
  Emerging Enterprises
  1155 15th St. NW
  Washington, DC 20005
  (800) 243-7232

U.S. Department of the Treasury
  Internal Revenue Service
  P.O. Box 25866
  Richmond, VA 23289
  (800) 829-3676

U.S. Small Business Administration
  409 Third St., SW
  Washington, DC 20416
  (800) 827-5722

Notes _____

A Concise Guide To Starting Your Own Business

Page A-2

Guide Overview

A concise overview of the complete guide to starting and operating a successful business.

The following topics are presented:

- Business Plan for Small Businesses.
- Getting Started
- Deciding Where To Start The Business
- Business Patronage Statistics
- Site Location
- Site Selection Criteria — Some General Questions.
- Choosing The Proper Method of Organization
- What Is A Corporation?
- Estimating Start-up Costs
- Preparing An Income Statement
- Preparing A Balance Sheet
- Marketing The Business
- Marketing Planning — An Outline for Marketing
- Advertising Media
- Management and Getting The Work Done
- Sample Organization Chart
- Summary of the Business Plan
- Guide Summary
- Reference Materials

Business Plan for Small Businesses

I. Type of Business

II. Location

III. Target Market

IV. Planning Process

V. Organizational Structure

VI. Staffing Procedures

VII. Control

VIII. Market Strategy

IX. Financial Planning

X. Budgeted Balance Sheet

XI. Budgeted Income Statement

XII. Budgeted Cash Flow Statement

XIII. Break-even Chart

Getting Started

Following is a list of what you need to accomplish to insure that your business endeavor will head in the right direction.

1. Define your educational background and work experience

2. Survey all basic types of businesses.

3. Define what type of business matches your experience and educational background.

4. Choose only the business that you would like to own and operate.

5. Define what products or services your business will be marketing.

6. Define who will be using your products/services.

7. Define why they will be purchasing your products/ services.

8. List all competitors in your marketing area.

Deciding Where to Start the Business

Will your business fulfill a need in the area you plan to bring your business to? This section provides you with some important information you need to examine before taking your ideas any further:

1. Decide where you want to live.

2. Choose several areas that would match your priorities.

3. Use the list that follows as a guide to see if your location will match the estimated population needed to support your business. The numbers which follow the type of business indicate the typical number of inhabitants per year.

Business Patronage Statistics

Food Stores
Grocery Stores 1,534
Meat and Fish
(Sea Food) Markets . . . 17,876
Candy, Nut, and
Confectionery Stores . . 31,409
Retail Bakeries 12,563
Dairy Products Stores . . . 41,587

Eating and Drinking
Restaurant, Lunch Rooms . 1,583
Cafeterias 19,341
Refreshment Places 3,622
Drinking Places 2,414

General Merchandise
Variety Stores 10,373
General Merchandise 9,837

Apparel/Accessories Stores
Women's Ready-To-
Wear Stores 7,102
Women's Accessory and
Specialty Stores 25,824
Men's and Boy's Clothing
and Furnishings 11,832
Family Clothing 16,890
Shoe Stores 9,350

Furniture, Home Furnishings, and Equipment Stores
Furniture Stores 7,210
Floor Covering 29,543
Drapery, Curtains, and
Upholstery Stores 62,585
House, Appliances 12,485
Radios and TV's 20,346
Record Shops 112,144
Musical Instruments 46,332

Building Materials, Hardware, and Farm Equipment Dealers
Lumber and other Building
Materials Dealers 8,124
Paint, Glass, and Wallpaper
Stores 22,454
Hardware Stores 10,206
Farm Equipment Dealers . 14,793

Automotive Dealers
Motor Vehicle Dealers,
New and Used Cars 6,000
Motor Vehicle Dealers,
Used Cars only 17,160
Tire, battery, and
Accessory Dealers 8,800

Boat Dealers 61,500

Household Trailer Dealers . 44,746

Gasoline Service Stations . . . 1,395

Miscellaneous
Antique and Secondhand
Stores 17,170
Book and Stationery Stores 28,580
Drugstores 4,268
Florists 13,531
Fuel Oil Dealers 25,000
Garden Supply Stores . . . 65,000
Gift, Novelty Shops 26,000
Hobby, Toy, and Game
Shops 61,000
Jewelry Stores 13,400
Optical Goods Stores 62,800
Sporting Goods Store 27,000

From *Starting and Managing a Small Business of Your Own, 1973;*
Small Business Administration, Washington, DC

Page A-6

Site Location

1. Define your number of inhabitants per store.

2. Locate several sites/locations that will match your inhabitants per stores.

3. Define population and its growth potential.

4. Define local ordinances and zoning regulations that you will need in order to start your type of business.

5. Define your trading area and all competitors in your trading area.

6. Define parking need, for your kind of business.

7. Define special needs, etc., lighting, heating, ventilation.

8. Define rental cost of site/location.

9. Define why customers will come to your site/location.

10. Define the future of your site/location as to population growth.

11. Define your space needs and match with site/location selection.

12. Define the image of your business and make sure it matches your site/location.

Site Selection Criteria — Some General Questions

- Is the site centrally located to reach my market?

- What is the transportation availability and what are the rates?

- What provisions for future expansion can I make:

- What is the topography of the site (slope and foundation)?

- What is the housing availability for workers and managers?

- What environmental factors (schools, cultural, community atmosphere) might affect my business and my employees?

- What will the quality of this site be in 5 years, 10 years, 25 years?

- What is my estimate of this site in relation to my major competitor?

- What other media are available for advertising? How many radio and television stations are there?

- Is the Quantity and quality of available labor concentrated in a given area in the city or town? If so, is commuting a way of living in that city or town?

- Is the city centrally located to my suppliers?

- What are the labor conditions, including such things as relationships with the business community and average wages and salaries paid?

- Is the local business climate healthy, or are business failures especially high in the area?

- What about tax requirements? Is there a city business tax? Income tax? What is the property tax rate? Is there a personal property tax? Are there other special taxes?

- Is the available police and fire protection adequate?

- Is the city or town basically well planned and managed in terms of such items as electric power, sewage, and paved streets and sidewalks?

Page A-8

Choosing the Proper Method of Organization

Listed below are legal forms of business available to the small business entrepreneur:

Sole Proprietorship

Advantages
- Simple to start
- All profits to owner
- Owner in direct control
- Easy entry and exit
- Taxed as individual

Disadvantages
- Unlimited liability
- "Jack-of-all-trades"
- Capital requirement limited
- Limited life
- Employee turn-over

Partnership

Advantages
- Easy to originate
- Credit rating
- Talent combination
- Legal Contract

Disadvantages
- Unlimited liability
- Misunderstandings
- Partner withdrawal
- Regulations

Corporation

Advantages
- Limited liability
- Expansion potential
- Transfer of ownership
- Retain employees

Disadvantages
- Double taxation
- Charter restrictions
- Employee motivation
- Legal regulations

What Is A Corporation?

A corporation is an artificial being, invisible, intangible, and existing only in contemplation of the law," wrote Chief Justice John Marshall. In other words, the corporation exists as a separate entity apart from its owners, the shareholders. It makes contracts; it is liable; it pays taxes. It is a "legal person".

The corporation is the most complex of the three major forms of business ownership. The corporation stands as a separate legal entity in the eyes of the law. The life of the corporation is independent of the owners' lives. Because the owners, called shareholders, are legally separate from the corporation, they can sell their interests in the business without affecting the continuation of the business. When a corporation is founded, it accepts the regulations and restrictions placed on it by the state in which it is incorporated and any other state in which it chooses to do business. Generally, the corporation must report its financial operations to the state's attorney general on an annual basis.

Page A-10

Estimating Start-up Costs

Item	Amount
Fixtures and Equipment	$ _____
Building & Land (If Needed)	_____
Store and/or Office Supplies	_____
Remodeling and Decorating	_____
Deposits on Utilities	_____
Insurance	_____
Installation of Fixtures	_____
Legal Fees	_____
Professional Fees	_____
Telephone	_____
Rental	_____
Salaries and Wages	_____
Inventory if Retailing	_____
Licenses and Permits	_____
Advertising and Promotion	_____
TOTAL Estimated Start-up Cost	$ _____

Preparing An Income Statement

What is an Income Statement?

The income statement shows the income received and the expenses incurred over a period of time. Income received (sales) comes essentially from the sales of the merchandise or service which your business is formed to sell. Expenses incurred are the expired costs that have been incurred during the same period of time.

Plan A Budgeted Income Statement For One Year

1. Project Total Sales
2. Estimate Total Expenditures
3. Example Listed Below for Income Statement

Percents	1	2	3	4	5	6	7	8	9	10	11	12
Sales												
Cost of Sales												
Gross Profit												
Expenditure												
Rent Expense												
Supplies												
Wages/Salaries												
Utilities												
Insurance												
Depreciation												
Interest												
Miscellaneous												
Net Profit												

Page A-12

Preparing A Balance Sheet

What is a Balance Sheet?

The balance sheet shows the assets, liabilities and owner's net worth in a business as of a given date.

- Assets are the things owned by your business, including both physical things and claims against others.
- Liabilities are the amounts owned to others, the creditors of the firm.
- Net worth or owner's equity is the owner's claim to the assets after liabilities are accounted for.

A Budgeted Balance Sheet For One Year

- List all your business property at their cost to you: these are your assets.
- List all debts, or what your business owes on all your property; these are your liabilities.
- Take your total property balance (Assets), and subtract the total amount you owe (Liabilities).
- The balance is what you own in your business called (Owner's equity).
- Add Total Liabilities (2) & Total Owner's Equity (3).
- Listed on the next page is an example of a balance sheet.

NAME OF BUSINESS
BALANCE SHEET
DATE

ASSETS

Current Assets
  Cash   _____
  Accounts Receivable   _____
Merchandise Inventories   _____
    TOTAL CURRENT ASSETS   _____

Fixed Assets
  Land   _____
  Building   _____
  Equipment   _____
    TOTAL FIXED ASSETS   _____
    TOTAL ASSETS   1). _____

LIABILITIES

Current Liabilities
  Accounts Payable   _____
  Note Payable   _____
  Payroll Taxes Payable   _____
    TOTAL CURRENT LIABILITIES   _____

Long-term Liabilities
  Mortgage Payable   _____
  Long-term Note   _____
    TOTAL LONG-TERM LIABILITIES   _____
    TOTAL LIABILITIES   2). _____

OWNER'S EQUITY

Proprietor's Capital   3). _____

    TOTAL LIABILITIES & OWNER'S EQUITY   (2 &3). _____

Page A-14

Marketing The Business

1. Define Your Market
   - Type of Customers
   - Age, Income, Occupation of your customers
   - Type of Trading Area

2. Promotion of Your Business
   - Advertising
   - Setting your Image

3. Customer Policy Plan
   - Develop a Customer Profile
   - Customer Services
   - Customer Needs

4. Pricing Your Products/Services
   - Know all your Costs
   - Know your Profit Margin
   - Know Competitor's Price
   - Know what Return you want on your Investment

5. Sales Promotion
   - Coupons
   - Contests
   - Displays
   - Demonstrations
   - Giveaways
   - Banners

6. Public Relations
   - Newspaper Article
   - Contact Trade Association
   - Radio Promotion
   - TV Promotion

7. Segmentation of your Market
   - Age
   - Occupation
   - Income
   - Location
   - Education
   - Hobbies

Marketing Planning

Outline for Marketing

I. Product/Service Concept:
    a. Name of product or service
    b. Descriptive characteristics of product or service
    c. Unit sales
    d. Analysis of market trends

II. Number of Customers in your Market Area:
    a. Profile of customers
    b. Average customer expenditure
    c. Total market

III. Your Market Potential:
    a. Total market divided by competition
    b. Total market multiplied by percent who will buy your product

IV. Needs of Customers:
    a. Identification
    b. Pleasure
    c. Social approval
    d. Personal interest
    e. Price

V. Direct Marketing Sources:
    a. Trade magazines
    b. Trade associations
    c. Small Business Administration (SBA)
    d. Government Publications
    e. Yellow pages
    f. Marketing directories

VI Customer Profile:
    a. Geographical
    b. Gender
    c. Age range
    d. Income brackets
    e. Occupation
    f. Educational level

Page A-16

Advertising Media

Medium	Market Coverage	Type of Audience
Daily newspaper	Single community or entire metro area: zoned editions sometimes available	General
Weekly newspaper	Single Community	Residents
Telephone Directory	Geographical area or occupational field served by the directory	Active shoppers for goods or services
Direct mail audience	Controlled by the advertiser	Controlled
Radio audience	Definable market area	Selected
Television audience	Definable market area surrounding TV Stations	Various
Outdoor	Entire metro area	General auto drivers
Magazine	Entire metro area or magazine region	Selected audience

Management and Getting the Work Done

1. Define your objective for starting your business.

2. Define your goals: profit growth for first three years.

3. Develop an organization chart of your business.

4. Define your personal needs.
   • Hiring proper employees
   • Training employees
   • Motivation

5. Define all responsibility for each person in your business.

6. Define all authority.
   • Who will hire and fire?
   • Who will select and train all personnel?
   • Who will keep the important records as to inventory, purchasing, sales records, cash records, etc.?

7. Define all laws and regulations that will be requirements for operating your business.

8. Review all duties and tasks with all your employees.

9. Write a summary of all the important tasks that you want to finish in your first year in business.

Sample Organization Chart

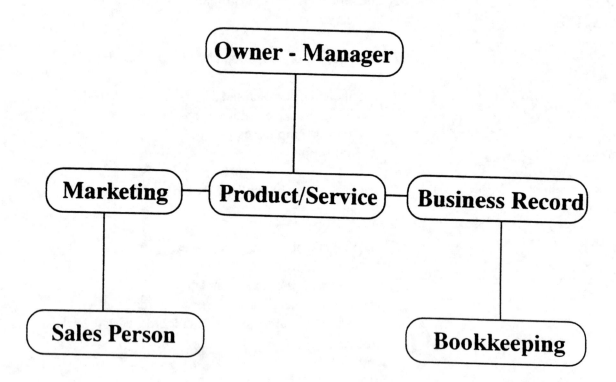

Summary of The Business Plan

Name of Business
BUSINESS PLAN
Date

1. Define your business
    -   Name all principals
    -   Address and phone number

2. Define your products or services

3. Define your market

4. Define your site or location

5. Advertising Plan
    -   Budget
    -   Media

6. Chart of Start-up cost

7. Worksheet of Income Statement
    -   Revenue/Income
    -   Expenses

8. Worksheet of Balance Sheet
    -   Assets (Property)
    -   Capital (Owner's Equity)
    -   Liabilities (Debts)

9. Personnel Outline
    -   Number of Employees
    -   Staffing & Training

10. Management Organization
    -   Organization Chart
    -   Evaluation Policy
    -   Job Profile

11. Special Statement
    -   3-Year Sales Schedule
    -   Cash Flow
    -   3-Year Expense Schedule

Appendix A
Summary

1. Contact your State Commerce Department for guidelines in starting your business.

2. Contact your City/County Clerk for guidelines in starting your business.

3. Contact all other Governmental Centers that will furnish you all the legal regulations and tax laws that will effect your business.
   - State Government
   - Internal Revenue Service
   - State Employment Security Commission
   - Department of Treasury
   - City Governmental Units

        a. Fire
        b. Police
        c. Zoning
        d. Building Permits
        e. Health
        f. Water & Sewage

4. Township Government
   - Local Legal Requirements
   - Local Taxes
   - Local Health Permits
   - Local Zoning Laws

Reference Materials

Management Aids Titles

Contact the

**Small Business Administration
P.O. Box 15434
Fort Worth, TX 76119**

for the following booklets:

- Number 2.025   Thinking About Going Into Business
- Number 2.010   Planning and Goal Setting For Business
- Number 1.016   Sound Cash Management
- Number 1.001   The A.B.C's. of Borrowing
- Number 1.008   Break-even Analysis
- Number 2.022   Business Plan For Service Firms
- Number 2.023   Business Plans for Retail Firms

Notes

Appendix B

HOUSEHOLD NEEDS

Many small business start-ups fail due to their inability to support their owners. Rarely do new businesses support their owners from the start. However, many individuals fail to recognize this fact. In addition, then, to a sound business plan, it is necessary for an owner to project the household cash needs month-by-month for the first three years of the business' operation. As a new business owner, you should be able to support yourself until your new business is able to support you in a manner to which you are accustomed.

MONTHLY HOUSEHOLD CASH NEEDS

Regular NON-BUSINESS Income
Spouse's salary _____
Investment income _____
Social security _____
Other income _____
Retirement benefits _____
Less taxes _____
Net monthly income _____

Regular Monthly Expenses

Housing
    Mortgage/Rent _____
    Utilities _____
    Homeowner's insurance _____
    Property taxes _____
    Home repairs _____

Living Expenses
    Groceries _____
    Telephone _____
    Tuition _____
    Transportation _____
    Meals _____
    Child care _____
    Medical expenses _____
    Clothing _____
    Personal _____

Insurance Premiums
    Life insurance _____
    Disability insurance _____
    Auto insurance _____
    Medical insurance _____

Debt Repayment
    Auto loans
    Consumer debt _____

Discretionary Expenses
    Entertainment _____
    Vacation _____
    Gifts _____
    Retirement contributions _____
    Investment savings _____
    Charitable contributions _____
    Dues, magazines, etc. _____
    Professional fees _____
    Other _____

Total Monthly Expenses _____

Monthly Surplus/Deficit _____

Total Year Surplus/Deficit _____
    (Monthly x 12)

Available Assets to Cover Deficit
    Checking accounts _____
    Savings accounts _____
    Money market accounts _____
    Personal credit lines _____
    Marketable securities _____
    Lump-sum retirement/
        severance _____
    Other assets _____

Total Assets _____

NEEDED RESERVES
    Total Assets-Deficit _____

PERSONAL FINANCIAL STATEMENT

This is a picture of your personal financial condition to date. It is a very important part of any loan application and/or interview, especially when a loan for a projected new business is under consideration.

PERSONAL FINANCIAL STATEMENT

_____ _____ , 19 _____

Assets
Cash   _____
Savings accounts   _____
Stocks, bonds, other securities   _____
Accounts/Notes receivable   _____
Life insurance cash value   _____
Rebates/Refunds   _____
Autos/Other vehicles   _____
Real estate   _____
Vested pension plan/Retirement accounts   _____
Other assets   _____
                                TOTAL ASSETS $ _____

Liabilities

Accounts payable   _____
Contracts payable   _____
Notes payable   _____
Taxes   _____
Real estate loans   _____
Other liabilities   _____
                            TOTAL LIABILITIES $ _____

TOTAL ASSETS $ _____

LESS TOTAL LIABILITIES $ _____

                                NET WORTH $ _____

BALANCE SHEET

A balance sheet is a current financial statement. It is a dollars and cents description of your business (existing or projected) which lists all of its assets and liabilities.

BALANCE SHEET

_____ _____ , 19 _____

	YEAR 1	YEAR II
Current Assets		
Cash		
Accounts receivable		
Inventory		
Fixed Assets		
Real estate		
Fixtures and equipment		
Vehicles		
Other Assets		
License		
Goodwill		
TOTAL ASSETS	$_____	$_____
Current Liabilities		
Notes payable (due within 1 year)	$_____	$_____
Accounts payable		
Accrued expenses		
Taxes owed		
Long-Term Liabilities		
Notes payable (due after 1 year)		
Other		
TOTAL LIABILITIES	$_____	$_____
NETWORTH (ASSETS minus LIABILITIES)	$_____	$_____

TOTAL LIABILITIES plus NET WORTH should equal ASSETS

PROFIT AND LOSS STATEMENT

A profit and loss statement is a detailed earnings statement for the previous full year (if you are already in business). Existing businesses are also required to show a profit and loss statement for the current period to the date of the balance sheet.

PROJECTED PROFIT AND LOSS STATEMENT

	Month 1	Month 2	Month 3	Month 4	Month 5	Month 6	Month 7	Month 8	Month 9	Month 10	Month 11	Month 12
Total Net Sales												
Cost of Sales												
GROSS PROFIT												
Controllable Expenses												
Salaries												
Payroll taxes												
Security												
Advertising												
Automobile												
Dues and subscriptions												
Legal and accounting												
Office supplies												
Telephone												
Utilities												
Miscellaneous												
Total Controllable Expenses												
Fixed Expenses Depreciation												
Insurance												
Rent												
Taxes and licenses												
Loan payments												
Total Fixed Expenses												
TOTAL EXPENSES												
NET PROFIT (LOSS) (before taxes)												

CASH FLOW PROJECTIONS

A cash flow projection is a forcast of the cash (checks or money orders) a business anticipates receiving and disbursing during the course of a month. Well managed, the cash flow should be sufficient to meet the cash requirements for the following month.

CASH FLOW PROJECTIONS

	Start-up or prior to loan	Month 1	Month 2	Month 3	Month 4	Month 5	Month 6	Month 7	Month 8	Month 9	Month 10	Month 11	Month 12	TOTAL
Cash (beginning of month														
Cash on hand														
Cash in bank														
Cash in investments														
Total Cash														
Income (during month)														
Cash sales														
Credit sales payment														
Investment income														
Loans														
Other cash income														
Total Income														
TOTAL CASH AND INCOME														
Expenses (during month														
Inventory or new material														
Wages (including owner's)														
Taxes														
Equipment expense														
Overhead														
Selling expense														
Transportation														
Loan repayment														
Other cash expenses														
TOTAL EXPENSES														
CASH FLOW EXCESS (end of month)														
CASH FLOW CUMULATIVE (Monthly)														

Appendix C

GETTING DOWN TO BUSINESS:

How to Start & Manage A Cosmetology Business

An Instructional Guide for
Creating A Small Business
by Jerre G. Lewis, M.A.
and Leslie D. Renn, M.S.

Notes

Planning a
Hair Styling Shop

Unit One: Planning a Hair Styling Shop

Goal: To help you plan your hair styling shop.

Objective 1: Describe the services, customers, and competition of a hair styling shop.

Objective 2: List three personal qualities the owner of a hair styling business might have.

Objective 3: List two ways to help your business "stand out" from its competition.

Objective 4: List two special legal requirements for running a hair styling shop.

Planning a Hair Styling Shop

Dinah's hair styling shop will be a small business. She will own the shop and make all the decisions. She will start with a small amount of money. She will work on her own, with no employees, and in one location. Like most small business owners, Dinah will need:

- drive and energy;
- problem solving ability; and
- ability to work well with people.

Services and Hair Care Products

The basic service Dinah plans to offer is hair care. This includes shampooing, cutting, waving, styling, and coloring. She may also decide to sell hair care products such as shampoo and conditioner to her customers.

The Importance of Personal Qualities

Dinah Simmons has some personal qualities that will be very important in making her small business a success. The case study shows she is:

- hard working and energetic;
- eager for the challenge of being her own boss;
- able to complete her cosmetology training and license requirements quickly;
- good at styling hair; and
- able to think clearly about setting goals.

Dinah may find that some of her personal qualities, however, rub other people the wrong way. For example, she may need to work harder at being:

- able to get along well with customers and employees; and
- flexible and willing to try new things.

Competing Successfully

Dinah has thought carefully about how to be competitive.

- She has gotten a good deal of hair care training and experience.
- She plans to advise each customer carefully about choices in hair styles and what is best for that person.
- She will make a special effort to attract people who can afford regular hair care. She hopes they will recommend her to their friends.

Legal Requirements

To run her own hair styling shop, Dinah must meet two types of legal requirements. She must have a license to give cosmetology service to customers. The license means she has gone through an approved beauty school program and passed the state licensing exam. She may also have to meet state or local requirements for running certain types of businesses. In most states, a cosmetologist needs one year of experience before opening or managing a beauty salon. The bureau of licenses in you state and city can tell you about requirements in your area.

SUMMARY

Beauty salons provide hair care and other services. The owner must decide what services to offer and how to attract and keep customers. It helps if a hair styling shop owner has energy and drive, and is clever at solving problems.

Choosing a Location

Unit Two: Choosing a Location

Goal: To help you choose a location for your business.

Objective 1: List three things to think about in deciding on service area for your bicycle store.

Objective 2: Pick the best building location for a bicycle store from three choices.

Choosing a Location

There are several things to think about when you choose a service area for your business. You should ask yourself these questions:

• Are there enough customers in the area?
• What is the competition?
• Can I be authorized to sell the brands I want in this area?
• Is this where I want to work?

You will also need to decide on a specific building for your store. These are things to think about.

• Will the location attract customers?
• Can I afford the rent?
• Is there enough space?

Choosing a good location is important to the success of a bicycle store. Some market research can pay off.

Competition

A bike store is in direct competition with other bike stores. If there is already a bike store in an area, you could still consider locating there, especially if there is a strong demand and you plan to offer different brands or a different service. However, if there are already two shops in an area, there probably is not enough business to open another one.

Specific Site

Consider these questions when you pick a specific site for your bicycle store.

Is it in a high traffic area? You should select a place that people notice. Being close to other stores or businesses can be helpful. You can count the number of people who walk and drive by to get an idea of the traffic flow. Also notice the type of people who go by and see if they are your target audience. Being next to a pizza place or a movie theater would be more likely to attract the customers you want rather than being next to an expensive restaurant. Being close to a college or high school can also be a good location.

SUMMARY

In deciding where to locate, you must decide if there are enough customers in an area to support a bike shop. You should take into consideration other bike shops in the area and what brands you could sell. In selecting a specific site, you will want to get the most convenient and attractive store at a price you can afford.

Getting Money
to Start

Unit Three: Getting Money to Start

Goal: To help you plan to get money to start your hair styling shop.

> **Objective 1:** Write a business description for your hair styling shop.
>
> **Objective 2:** Fill out a form showing how much money you need to borrow to start your hair styling shop.

DINAH GETS MONEY TO START HER HAIR STYLING SHOP

Dinah took stock of her finances. She had about $2,000 in personal savings to invest. She thought how much more she would need.

Dinah spent a good deal of time figuring out her starting expenses. She planned to work alone. So she did not have to pay out any salary. Dinah made a list of her expenses.

```
Rent (3 months) . . . . . . . . . . . . . . . . . . . . . . . . . . . . $1,500
Repairs & Remodeling . . . . . . . . . . . . . . . . . . . . . . . 300
Equipment & Furniture . . . . . . . . . . . . . . . . . . . . . . 1,700
Supplies . . . . . . . . . . . . . . . . . . . . . . . . . . . . . . . . . . . 900
Advertising . . . . . . . . . . . . . . . . . . . . . . . . . . . . . . . . . 350
Other: telephone; license; insurance . . . . . . . . . . . . . 250

    TOTAL . . . . . . . . . . . . . . . . . . . . . . . . . . . . . . . . $5,000
```

Dinah had about $2,000 of her own savings to invest. That meant she needed to borrow $3,000. She called an officer at the bank about her need to get a loan. The officer said she should bring in her statement of financial need and a description of her planned business as soon as possible. The bank would be able to process her loan application.

Dinah began writing her business description. It clearly and briefly described Dinah's plan to offer a full range of hair dressing and hair styling services and to sell high-quality hair care products. She gave an estimate of the number of beauty salons and barbershops in Naperville offering similar services. She pointed out the number of potential customers for these services. And she wrote down the percent of this market that she hoped to attract. It was three to six percent.

Dinah summarized her plan to attract professional women and wives of professionals by providing personal consulting advice.

Choosing a Money Source

Each money source has good and bad points. Having money saved up to help start your own business is wise. It shows you have the ability to handle money. It makes you less dependent on others. Lenders also are more impressed if you have some of your own money to invest.

Statement of Financial Need

Each dollar amount in Dinah's statement of financial need is an estimate, or best guess, of what she needs. Perhaps she could get by with a smaller amount of start-up money. On the other hand, her estimate for repair and remodeling seems low. Dinah's cousin said he could do some repair work in his spare time. If she spends $100 for materials, for example, only $200 is left to pay her cousin for his time. Most construction and repair workers earn a high hourly rate. So $200 will probably pay for only a few days of work.

<u>Cosmetology equipment</u> . . . . $ 400
This would include supplies such as curlers, a blow dryer, permanent wave rods, spray bottles, a hot comb, gloves, a neck strip and holders, combs and brushes, clips and rollers, hair pins, and shampoo and comb-out capes.

<u>Furnishings</u> $1,200
This would include needed furniture such as a styling chair, a shampoo bowl, a dryer chair, a comb-out station, a booth for styling/tinting, a reception desk, a reception chair, two waiting room chairs, and a coffee table.

<u>Cleaning equipment</u> . . . . $ 100
This would include supplies such as a broom, mop, and dustpan, a toilet brush, sponges, toilet paper, and soap and cleansers. These three subtotals added up to $1,700, the amount Dinah had put on her expense list for Equipment and Furniture.

<u>Cosmetology supplies</u> . . . . $ 900
This would include items such as shampoos, color rinses special rinses, hair colors, lighteners, conditioners, permanent wave solution, and hair spray. This amount appeared on Dinah's expense list under "Supplies."

Here is Dinah's completed statement of financial need that she used in applying for a bank loan.

STATEMENT OF FINANCIAL NEED	
<u>Starting Expenses</u>	<u>Money on Hand</u>
Rent (3 months) . . . . $ 1,500	Cash on Hand . . . . $ 2,000
Repairs and Renovations 300	Gifts or Personal Loans . . . . -0-
Equipment and Furniture 1,700	Investments by Others . . . . <u>-0-</u>
Supplies 900	
Advertising 350	
Other . . . . <u>250</u>	
TOTAL . . . . $ 5,000	TOTAL . . . . $ 2,000

TOTAL STARTING EXPENSES . . $ 5,000
TOTAL MONEY ON HAND . . . . . <u>2,000</u>
TOTAL LOAN MONEY NEEDED . . <u>$ 3,000</u>

Business Description

Dinah's planning for her business was very thorough. In her business description, she described her ideas for an appealing business image. But something was left out that the lending institution will want to know. This was her plan for locating her business. The business description should state that Dinah plans to locate her beauty salon in a neighborhood location that is:

• close to shopping, parking and public transportation;

• set up to house a beauty salon with minimum repair and remodeling; and

• in an area where no other beauty salons are in business.

This information will help the bank decide whether Dinah's plan for her small business is sound.

SUMMARY

To apply for a loan, you need a business description and a statement of financial need. A beauty shop business description explains the services to be offered and the types of customers the business will attract. It should also highlight things that will make this business stand out. To write a statement of financial need, you must estimate start-up expenses and money on hand. The difference between these figures shows how much you need to borrow.

Notes

Being in Charge

Unit Four: Being in Charge

Goal: To help you learn about managing work and people in a hair styling shop.

Objective 1: Plan how to get workers for all the necessary tasks of your business by hiring employees, contracting for services, or both.

Objective 2: Pick the best person for a specific job in your business.

Objective 3: Describe the types of training you would give employees depending on their jobs and backgrounds.

Being in Charge

Developing a list of business tasks helped Dinah sort out the tasks she wanted to do herself from those she wanted someone else to do. In cosmetology, as in most businesses, you can divide the work a number of different ways. But somebody must be responsible for every important task.

Dividing the Work

Dinah is already thinking about hiring people to do some of her business tasks. So Dinah comes up with another idea. "Some of my customers could definitely use help with their nails. If I hired a manicurist, I could offer an extra service and make more money." But the thought of supervising and paying employees does not appeal to Dinah. She prefers to hire people who work independently. Then she can get help just when she needs it on a short-term basis. Or she can contract for services on a regular basis.

Training Employees

To what extent will Dinah be responsible for training her two new business associates? With Lydia, the housecleaner, Dinah assumes Lydia knows how to use housecleaning equipment and supplies. She will trust Lydia on how to get things clean, for the most part. All Dinah plans to offer in terms of training is to tell Lydia what she wants cleaned, and how often. She hopes that Lydia can work out a detailed list of tasks and follow it herself, without much supervision. Dinah, though, must check Lydia's work carefully and tell her if something is not okay.

Dinah might have hired an employee to do hair care. Then Dinah would probably have been more active in training that person. She would have worked out with each employee:

• the specific tasks to be carried out;

• the material to use; and

• how to do the work--for example, whether to leave the curlers in for 15 minutes or just for 10 minutes on a first permanent.

SUMMARY

Obtaining needed services takes some effort. Now you know some things to think about in contracting for services. You also know what to consider in hiring and training an employee.

Notes _____

Organizing
the Work

Unit Five: Organizing the Work

Goal: To help you learn how to keep track of the work of a hair styling shop.

Objective 1: Fill out a form listing the tasks and materials needed to serve customers of a hair styling salon.

Objective 2: Develop a daily work schedule for a cosmetologist.

Organizing the Work

In a hair styling business you need to organize your work to get everything done smoothly. This means keeping track of your customers' appointments. It also means organizing the other jobs you'll need to get done--like ordering supplies, paying bills, and studying about new styles and hair care techniques.

Record of Special Services

Dinah fills out cards for customers to whom she gives permanents and other special treatments (like frosting and dyeing jobs.) This helps her know which beauty products she has used and the success she has had. Every customer has different hair. Some hair responds better to one permanent wave solution, other hair to another. Curlers have to be left in longer for some customers than others, too. Her "special services" card looks like this:

Customer _____

Date   Special Services   Comments

_____

_____

_____

SUMMARY

A hair styling shop owner needs to be well organized. As a beauty salon owner, you will spend a great deal of time making and changing appointments. A daily work schedule will help you arrange your time to get everything done. Keeping a record of special services given to regular customers helps you give them the best hair care--time after time.

Notes

Setting Prices

Unit Six: Setting Prices

Goal: To help you decide how to set prices for your hair styling shop.

Objective 1: List factors that affect the prices of hair care services.

Objective 2: Pick the best price for a specific hair care service.

Setting Prices

Hair styling shop owners must think about a number of thing when setting the price of a services:

- cost of supplies;
- operating expenses;
- profit;
- demand; and
- competitors' prices.

To decide how much to charge for a Flexiperm, Dinah thought about each one of these things.

Operating Expenses

Dinah had to charge enough for services to cover the expenses of running the salon. She had to pay her lease, keep her equipment in good condition, and pay a monthly water and electricity bill. Dinah figured that she needed to charge at least $5.00 for one hour of services just to pay her operating expenses. If she had other beauticians whom she had to pay, Dinah would have had to figure their wages into her operating expenses, too.

SUMMARY

Several things affect the price of cosmetology services. Operating expenses, cost of supplies, and profit for the owner must be covered. Customer demand and competition form other salons also affect how much you can charge. For example, if demand for a service is high and competition is low, it is possible to charge more. In this unit we discussed prices of a permanent. Different services have different prices, however. You should charge more for services that take more time, skill, or materials.

Advertising and Selling

Unit Seven: Advertising and Selling

Goal: To help you learn ways to advertise and sell the services of a hair styling shop.

Objective 1: List ways that a hair styling shop promotes, or "sells," its services.

Objective 2: Pick one way to advertise a hair styling shop.

Objective 3: Design a printed ad for a hair styling shop.

Advertising and Selling

Advertising is important for all businesses. Offering good services in a friendly setting is not enough. If no one knows about you, you won't get customers, and your business may fail. Once you attract people through advertising, you must keep them coming to your shop time after time. This means "selling" your services through your hair styling skills and your friendly service.

When your shop opens, you should plan a large advertising campaign. Later you can do less. You should advertise every month, however, to stay successful. You must follow the steps of good selling every time you see a customer.

How to Spread the Word

Of all the kinds of advertising you can use, the following are probably best for a hair styling shop:

• Yellow Pages ads;

• ads in local newspapers;

• fliers and business cards; and

• word of mouth.

Why Advertise Every Month?

Suppose you have enough regular customers to fill up your calendar. You may think that you no longer need to advertise. This is not true. You should advertise every month to:

• encourage first-time customers to come back;

• remind regular customers that you're "still around;"

• attract new customers to replace ones who move away;

• inform people of your new address or new services;

• announce special prices; and

• bring in customers for newly hired stylists.

How to Sell

Good cosmetologists "sell" their services. They show their customers that they understand their needs. Dinah "sells" her business every day.

• She is as polite and helpful as she can be.

• She answers questions and gives advice.

• She makes customers feel special.

SUMMARY

There are many ways to advertise and "sell" your hair styling salon. Advertising tells people about your shop and gets them to come see you. Your high-quality hair care and your friendly services are ways to keep your customers once they come in. Good service also makes your customers want to tell their friends about your shop.

Notes

Keeping
Financial Records

Unit Eight: Keeping Financial Records

Goal: To help you learn how to keep financial records for a hair styling shop.

> **Objective 1:** Fill out a sales slip for a sale in your hair styling shop.
>
> **Objective 2:** Fill out a daily cash sheet for money received and paid out in one day.

Keeping Financial Records

A hair styling shop owner must keep close track of income and expenses. Dinah needs good financial records to know how her business is doing. She also needs them for financial reports required by the government. Two of the forms that Dinah fills out daily are the sales slip and the daily cash sheet.

The daily records of a business are periodically summarized and organized into forms that show how the business is doing, such as a balance sheet and a profit/loss statement. You will learn about profit/loss statements in the next unit. If you do go into business for yourself, get the advice of a bookkeeper or accountant about how to complete a balance sheet.

SUMMARY

Hair styling shops use sales slips to record purchases from customers. They use daily cash sheets to record total cash receipts and payments each day. Daily figures are added up at the end of each month.

Notes

Keeping Your Business Successful

Unit Nine: Keeping Your Business Successful

Goal: To help you learn how to keep your styling shop successful.

Objective 1: Figure out the net profit, profit ratio, and expense ratio for your business.

Objective 2: State one way your business could increase its profits.

Objective 3: State one way your business could change its services to increase sales.

Profit/Loss Statement

The yearly profit/loss statement is one record you can use to check your business' health. The profit/loss statement lists your yearly revenues, cost of goods sold, and gross profits. Revenues is the total income received from customers. The sum of all costs, expenses, and net profits equals total revenues. Cost of goods sold is the amount you spend for beauty supplies for the shop and "take-home" products sold to customers. Gross profit equals revenues minus cost of goods sold.

On the profit/loss statement, all your operating expenses are also listed. These include all the money you spend to keep the shop open every day (salaries, rent, utilities, advertising, insurance, etc.). In Dinah's case, she included the wages paid to her accountant and house cleaner under "other."

Net profit is the reward for all your hard work. Net profit covers your salary as the owner and money to expand your business. To figure your net profit, subtract expenses from gross profit. You should also look at your profit ratios and expense ratios. All of these appear on Dinah's profit/loss statement below.

TWO-YEAR PROFIT/LOSS STATEMENT

	Year 2		Year 3	
	$	%	$	%
Revenues	$ 42,000	100%	$ 50,000	100%
Cost of Goods Sold	4,620		6,000	
Gross Profit	$ 37,380		$ 44,000	
Expenses				
Rent	6,000		6,000	
Utilities	1,500		2,000	
Advertising	1,160		1,700	
Insurance	500		800	
Other	3,860	31%	5,500	
TOTAL	$ 13,020		$ 16,000	____%
Net Profit (before Dinah's salary and income taxes)	$ 24,360	58%	$28,000	____%

Keeping Your Profits High

To keep profits high, you should try some of the following:

• increase sales of your more profitable products and services;

• add new products and services;

• raise prices;

• reduce costs of goods sold; and

• reduce operating expenses.

Often you must do several things to stay successful. Look at all parts of your profit/loss statement. Study your customers and trends in the beauty field. Then figure out the best changes for your business.

SUMMARY

A small business owner must keep track of cash flow. Comparing revenues to expenses tells you the net profit for your business. Dividing net profit by revenues tells you the profit ratio. Small business owners must keep their profits and profit ratios high and their expenses and expense ratios low to be successful.

Increasing sales, raising prices, and reducing expenses are ways to improve profits. A hair styling shop owner can improve services or add new products and services to increase sales.

HAIR STYLING SHOP SUMMARY

This module has been about owning a small hair styling shop. People with training in cosmetology can start similar businesses.

To start a small business, you need to do lots of planning. First you have to be sure that owning a small business is right for you. Then you have to decide what services to offer, how to compete, and what legal requirements to meet.

To pick a good location, you have to find out if customers would come to your shop. Then you have to get money to start. That means showing a banker that your idea is a good one.

Being in charge means dividing the work and hiring good workers. Then you must keep track of jobs to be done and who will do them.

Setting prices means figuring out the lowest price you can charge to meet your expenses and also the highest price you can charge and still be competitive. To do this you need information on your expenses and on your competition's prices.

Advertising is how you get customers. It's an important "investment" in your business. A satisfied customer is the very best advertisement you can have.

You should keep good financial records so you will know how the business is doing. Then you can decide if you can expand your business or if you need to cut it back.

In order to own and operate a successful hair styling shop, you need training in cosmetology work experience, and the special business management skills we have covered in this module. If you have not had a course in cosmetology, you should take one before deciding to own this kind of business. You can learn business management skills through business classes, experience, or by using the advice and example of an expert.

You may not make a lot of money by owning a hair styling shop. However, you will have the personal satisfaction of being responsible for your business and making your own decisions. Think about how important these things are to you in considering whether you should start your own hair styling shop.

Notes

Appendix D

INSURANCE CHECKLIST

TYPE OF INSURANCE	PURCHASE	DO NOT PURCHASE
PROPERTY INSURANCE:		
Fire	_____	_____
Windstorm	_____	_____
Hail	_____	_____
Smoke	_____	_____
Explosion	_____	_____
Vandalism	_____	_____
Water Damage	_____	_____
Glass	_____	_____
LIABILITY INSURANCE	_____	_____
WORKERS' COMPENSATION	_____	_____
BUSINESS INTERRUPTION	_____	_____
DISHONESTY:		
Fidelity	_____	_____
Robbery	_____	_____
Burglary	_____	_____
Comprehensive	_____	_____
PERSONAL:		
Health	_____	_____
Life	_____	_____
Key Personnel	_____	_____

Getting Down to Business...

How to Start
& Manage
A Cosmetology
Business

An Instructional Guide for Creating A Small Business
by Jerre G. Lewis, M.A.
& Leslie D. Renn, M.S.

Notes

Cosmetology

In past years, cosmetology salons (beauty salons) have provided services primarily for female patrons. Because of recent changes in hair fashions, salons now attract male patrons.

All states require that the manager of a beauty salon be licensed to practice hairdressing and cosmetology. Since the requirements for such a license vary, check with the Bureau of Licenses in the state and city in which the salon is to be operated. Knowledge of Federal and State regulations and ethical business practices is recommended by the National Hairdressers and Cosmetologists Association.

Capital Requirements and Operating Ratios: A profile survey of the beauty salon owner reveals most salons have gone into business with less than $4,000 capital. The amount of capital needed depends upon the location of the salon, the decor, and the type and amount of equipment. Keep enough cash on hand to operate the business until a substantial clientele is well established.

Capital Investment: Requirements for establishing a beauty salon depend upon the type and quality of equipment and decor necessary to project the desired image. Shampoo stations and chairs, styling stations and hair dryers are the major investments. If the landlord provides plumbing and electrical installations, this will reduce capital investment by the owner. If the owner is required to provide all decor, plumbing, electrical, air conditioning and heating equipment, the investment will be greater. This addition to the leasehold can be amortized over the period of the lease for leasehold improvements.

The beauty salon employee is generally compensated on a commission basis ranging from 40 to 50 percent of gross receipts for services. The salon owner is also responsible for the various State and Federal taxes for its employees. Salon owners must also project a salary for themselves.

Beauty salon operating expenses (by percentages) as reported by industry members, explains operating costs. These operating expenses have fluctuated throughout the years with net profits varying within a two (2) percent range.

Salon Operating Expenses (by percentage):

Services Expenses	
Salaries and Commissions (including owner's)	57.48%
Rent	4.70%
Supplies	6.39%
Advertising and Promotion Costs	
Depreciation of Salon Equipment, Fixtures, and Furniture	2.29%
Laundry	0.99%
Utilities (light, heat, power, water)	2.06%
Repairs and Salon Maintenance	1.56%
Insurance Costs (salon & personal liability)	1.80%
Telephone Expenses	1.01%
Interest and Carrying Charges	.093%
License Fees and taxes (such as personal property, payroll, etc.)	3.32%
Legal and Bookkeeping Services	1.15%
Dues, Magazines, Travel & Education	2.19%
Fringe Benefit Expenses	1.42%
Total Expenses	90.73%
Profit	9.27%
Total:	100.00%

Marketing: Four major requirements for a successful salon operation are location, image, ability of cosmetologists, and price structure for services.

Industry Future: The beauty industry is a personal service-oriented business and has experienced continued growth. The growth potential is based upon the following: in recent years statistics show 36 percent of all women over 18 years of age visited a beauty salon during a four-week period, leaving a potential of 64 percent who may want beauty services.

Notes

Special Appendix

Web Site Marketing

Business Web Site
an
Effective Marketing Tool

More than 100 million people use the Internet each day. A website offers help in marketing your small business. Your web site can help level the playing field for small businesses who compete with big businesses. It can enable small business to expand their business nationally or internationally.

What makes a good web site?

A good web site shows by doing; it proves rather than states. Instead of making claims, it provides evidence.

Evidence can take several forms:

- Case Studies showing how your efforts solved a previous client's problems.

- Testimonials from satisfied clients.

- Reprints of articles you've written or reviews of your work.

Education, however, remains the best way to establish credibility. To the extent prospects leave your web site better informed about your product or service, the easier it is to gain their respect (and their purchase order).

Three steps to creating your own business web site.

Today's tools make web publishing accessible to small businesses without programming experience. For example, Microsoft® Publisher 97 includes PageWizard design assistants, web deign elements and design checkers to help your build a workable web site.

Step one:

Choose a structure and a look. Your site should be structured and designed to best tell your story. But where do you start? Using the Page Wizard, you can choose from pre-designed options that can later be customized so that establishing a structure and "look" is easy.

Step two:

Tell your story. Next, simply select the sample headlines and text provided and replace them with words that describe what you have to offer.

Step three:

Check your work and post your site. The design in Publisher 97 goes through your web site element by element, identifying potential problems. Then, the web publishing wizard guides you through the process of posting your web site on the local Internet service provider or on-line service of your choice.

Remember, with millions of web sites, you may have to market your web site as well as your small business to get traffic for your business. The web site can be an inexpensive way of effectively building your small business.

10 tips for Web Site Online Marketing

1. Put up a simple web page.
2. Use a name that will attract people
3. Give away advice and information
4. Have lots of e-mail correspondence
5. Provide customized pages for users.
6. Visit user groups
7. Get on mailing lists
8. Arrange links with related sites
9. Make sure you're in every possible directory
10. Do not "SPAM"

INDEX